# WHEN YOU'RE MOM NO. 2

# When You're Mom No. 2

*A Word of Hope for Stepmothers*

Dr. Beth E. Brown

Servant Publications
Ann Arbor, Michigan

Vine Books is an imprint of Servant Publications especially
designed to serve Evangelical Christians.

Published by Servant Publications
P.O. Box 8617
Ann Arbor, Michigan 48107

Cover design by Michael Andaloro
Cover photo by Doug Larime

91 92 93 94 95  10 9 8 7 6 5 4 3 2 1

Printed in the United States of America
ISBN 0-89283-719-5

### Library of Congress Cataloging-in-Publication Data

Brown, Beth E., 1946-
    When you're mom no. 2 : a word of hope for stepmothers
/ Beth E.
        p.  cm.
    Includes bibliographical references.
    ISBN 0-89283-719-5
    1. Stepmothers—United States. 2. Stepfamilies—United
States. 3. Stepmothers—United States—Religious life.
    I. Title: When you're mom number two.
HQ759.92.B76   1991
306.874—dc20                                   91-18653
                                                    CIP

*to*
*my husband,*
*Don,*

*and to*
*all our children:*
*Rick*
*Sharon*
*Steve*
*Kayleen*
*David*
*Amy*
*April*

# Contents

*stant lack of privacy, they must also adjust to an increased work load in caring for a family. How self-acceptance, communication, and a hopeful attitude can see you through.*

*The secret to a happy stepfamily is a happy marriage. How to build the best marriage you can through good communication, shared decision-making, and ongoing romance.*

*As you think about where to live, practicality is only one consideration. Emotional cost is another. Changing things upsets the kids, leaving things the same upsets you. Making wise choices may not be as hard as it seems.*

*As important as it is to understand and accept your stepfamily's history, you can create fresh traditions which will develop into new and rewarding family memories.*

*Some stepmothers are afraid that discipline will endanger their relationships with the children. Some fathers feel too guilty about their remarriage to discipline their children. Both parents need to value discipline and agree on Mom No. 2's role in the family.*

*New babies typically bring a fresh unity to the stepfamily. Advice about having children, bringing the baby home, balancing the needs of the children, and involving stepchildren in the baby's care.*

*Change is just about the only constant in our lives. A healthy stepfamily will move through several predictable transitions.*

# Acknowledgements

I THANK GOD FOR PROVIDING the following friends and family who encouraged me in writing this book:

- The Board of Trustees of Denver Seminary who granted me a sabbatical leave that I might research and write this book.
- Diane Barnhart, my friend and able research assistant, for her thorough work and continued interest in the project.
- Alyce Van Til, a faithful friend, who willingly read and corrected the original manuscript.
- Beth Feia, whom I've come to know and respect as an invaluable editor and to love as a friend. She taught me much about the art of writing, and also the ministry of writing.
- The many women who freely shared their stories with me—both their successes and disappointments in stepmothering.
- My parents, Ernest and Myra Hollenbach, who pray for me daily, and whose friendship keeps me going.
- My children, including Amy and April who, in their weekly phone calls home from college, always checked on the book's progress; Sharon, who patiently answered my barrage of questions in lengthy long-distance phone calls; and especially Kayleen and David, who generously shared their personal memories and insights into our family's life together.
- My husband, Don, who lovingly expressed confidence in my ability to write this book, who carefully read each word, who made helpful positive suggestions, and who graciously agreed to write an Afterword as the husband of a Mom No. 2.

# Introduction

THOUGH BUNDLED UP AGAINST THE BITTER, cold February night air, I shivered and moved closer to the warmth of my new husband as he drove us to the Buffalo, New York airport. Rick, my husband's oldest son, was due in on an early evening flight from Eugene, Oregon. Don and I had only been married two months and I was going to meet my stepson for the very first time. He was eighteen years old and I was just twenty-one. What would Rick think of me? I shivered again. Was it from the cold or was I shaken by my own fears?

Some of the younger children in the back seat were excited at the thought of seeing their big brother again. They had not seen Rick since he had gone to live with his grandparents and to attend college after his mother's death. I was grateful for the sound of their voices and their laughter because it allowed me to retreat into the privacy of my own swirling thoughts and emotions. During that all-too-short drive along the cold, snowy streets to the airport, Don entered into lively conversation with the children. He was obviously just as eager as they to have the family all together again.

This was my family now, but somehow I felt like an intruder. I was the outsider looking in on a private family moment. In the middle of a family reunion, I was a stranger in the crowd. I loved my new husband deeply and I wanted to love and to be loved by all his children. But Rick had not been around when Don and I met, fell in love, and married. Would he even like me?

We arrived at the airport and walked the short distance to the gate where Rick's plane would be coming in. After only a few moments, the passengers from Eugene began to flood into the chilly concourse. Rick was wildly greeted by his four excited brothers and sisters who gathered around him. Next, he hugged his father. Then he turned to me.

I'll never forget that next moment. This six-foot-three, good-looking eighteen-year-old, looked down at me. A warm grin spread across his face and he said... "Hi, Mom!"

That moment of acceptance from Rick was a precious gift for which I will always be inexpressibly grateful. It could have been so different. He could have been hostile, or perhaps worse yet, indifferent. Instead, he chose to accept me. I will never forget that moment twenty-three years ago in the Buffalo airport when ice and snow and cold turned to warmth.

Most stepmothers can recall similar feelings of apprehension, insecurity, intrusion, and awkwardness. When I married Don Brown, a widower with five children, I entered uncharted territory with little to guide me. No one had prepared me for what it meant to be a "stepmother." No one had defined this role for me. My faith and commitment to Jesus Christ were my only preparation for the challenge, and he was good to me.

I don't think my lack of preparation was unusual. You may be a Mom No. 2 or considering becoming Mom No. 2. Maybe you're a man thinking of asking someone to marry you and become Mom No. 2 to your children. It's my prayer that you'll find hope and help as I share my own story with you. May you also be encouraged by the stories of other stepmothers who willingly told of their own experiences as Mom No. 2. Throughout this book, I have changed their names to protect their family privacy.

Many stepmothers are struggling. These struggles can be eased by understanding the challenges of stepmothering, becoming more realistic in our expectations, listening to and sharing one another's experiences, and realizing that in a very real sense stepmothering can be a ministry to which God has called some of us.

Some of the statistics are grim. Half of all marriages during the last two decades are projected to end in divorce. And that's not all the bad news. Paul Cullen, a marriage and family expert, points out that "second marriages fail at a higher rate than first marriages, usually within four years... the rate is said to be as high as sixty-five percent."[1] Currently, close to thirteen percent of all families are stepfamilies: almost half the result of divorce; others from families of unmarried mothers; and the smallest group is formed through the death of a parent.[2] If present trends continue, Cullen reports, "in the next five years, the United States will have more single-parent and stepparent families than traditional families."[3]

According to Frank Furstenberg, Jr., from the University of Pennsylvania, "most young children who see their parents' marriage dissolve are likely to enter a stepfamily before they reach adulthood." He continues, "It is estimated that forty percent of all children will encounter divorce, and about one in four will live with a stepparent before they reach the age of sixteen. If we calculated as well the existence of stepparents not living with the child, *probably a third of all children growing up today will be part of a stepfamily before they reach adulthood.*"[4] Equally startling is David and Bonnie Juroe's prediction that "if current trends continue at the present pace, by the end of this century more mothers and fathers will be parenting stepchildren than their own!"[5]

Dealing with the problems of stepparenting demands more than just dealing with the increasing numbers. It means coming to grips with complexities that stepfamilies present: the interrelationships between and among the remarried parent, the stepparent, the stepchildren, and half-brothers and half-sisters who all bring their own expectations and experiences to this unique family.

When You're Mom No. 2 focuses on the experience of the stepmother and her relationship to her stepchildren. I have chosen to limit myself to stepmothering because the role of the stepmother is typically more difficult and challenging than the role of the stepfather, in part because of differing expectations by society.

Stepmothering continues to be the more challenging role mainly because society still regards the woman as the nurturing parent and judges the adjustment of the family by how well or how poorly the substitute female parent seems to be faring.[6] Although most people agree that the role of the stepmother is more difficult and demanding than the role of the stepfather, paradoxically it also seems to promise a greater potential for success.[7]

Stepmothering is tough work because a stepmother typically spends more time with the children than a stepfather, even if she works outside of the home. However, although she usually has more responsibility than her husband for homemaking and child care, that very fact causes her to fit into a recognized and needed role more quickly than would be the case for a stepfather. The stepmother's advantage is that her caregiving provides an opportunity to establish warm relationships that may take a stepfather much longer.

In addition, the Christian stepmother may find that her faith in Christ provides much needed hope, patience, and love in building a Christian home. In Romans 12:12, the apostle Paul encourages us to be joyful in hope. A relationship with Christ can bring joyful hope to the ministry of a stepmother, helping her to see beyond the daily challenges, strengthening her for the task, and deepening her love for her new family.

Stepfamilies pose a direct challenge to the notion that only families related by blood can be happily adjusted families.

Pulled and jerked by multiple relationships from both within and without the new family, there is little question that the challenge to build a new sense of family commitment can be a formidable one. But it can be done. The Christian stepfamily has some advantage in that difficult task.

When I first became a stepmother, I felt very alone in my new role. I want you to know that you are not alone. Many women, all around you, are sharing this experience of stepmothering. Christ, too, wants to be present with you in your new life. It's my hope that sharing the experiences of others and learning from what they have to teach us will be an encouragement to you WHEN YOU'RE MOM NO. 2.

# ONE

# The Wicked Stepmother

*Long ago, in a faraway kingdom, there lived a lovely young Princess named Snow White. Her stepmother, the Queen, was cruel and vain. She hated anyone whose beauty rivaled her own—and she watched her stepdaughter with angry, jealous eyes.*

**Snow White and the Seven Dwarfs**

STEPMOTHERS ARE NEVER PICTURED as heroines in common folklore. What little girl, when listening to childhood fairy tales, has ever longed to grow up to be a stepmother? Snow White's stepmother was so horrible that she gave her lovely stepdaughter a poisoned apple. Cinderella's stepmother was deceptive, selfish, and cruel, and forced her stepdaughter to live in the attic, wear old rags, and do all the housework. Hansel and Gretel's wicked stepmother plotted to take the children deep into the forest and lose them there. Their story ends happily as Hansel and Gretel escape, find their way home, see their loving father again, and also learn that their wicked stepmother is dead!

When I heard those stories as a young child, I fantasized that I was Snow White, Cinderella, and Gretel! But now I find that I have grown up to be the "wicked stepmother!"

Many women in stepfamilies have told me about the shameful stigma wrought by such fairy tales. Suzanne is a forty-eight-year-old whose father divorced her natural mother when she was five. When he remarried, he told his three children to call her "Mommy." Suzanne's father wanted the family to be "normal" and disliked the "stepmother" stigma. He felt that his family life was "nobody's business." Suzanne grew to love her stepmother very much, but she was bothered by the subterfuge and secrecy, sensing that something was wrong about having a stepmother. She grew up feeling that she was, in her words, "living a lie." She described herself as a compliant child who didn't dare to reveal this forbidden information. She was so persuaded not to disclose this deep, dark secret, that when she married, she didn't even tell her husband that her "mother" was *really* her stepmother.

One day, Suzanne's neighbor mentioned that she was going to visit her own stepmother, Suzanne was shocked at the mention of the awful "s" word! She couldn't believe that anyone would *talk* about having a stepmother! For the first time in her life, at the age of twenty-five, Suzanne admitted that the mother who had raised her was her stepmother and not her natural mother. She went home and shared the "awful secret" with her husband and experienced unbelievable release by talking openly about the stepmother whom she loved.

Denying the reality of the divorce and remarriage had created problems for all three children in her parents' family. It could have contributed to the fact that Suzanne's older sister eventually took her own life. Suzanne ended our conversation by telling me, "If I had not become a Christian, I'd be an emotional mess. The Lord helped me to go and talk to my parents." Though her parents were angry with Suzanne's new openness, she had found sweet release.

Suzanne's story illustrates how taboo the whole subject of stepfamilies was just a few years ago. Even today, Emily and John Visher, well-known authors and researchers on the stepfamily, note that "... usually the word 'stepfamily' conjures up a negative image. While the word 'family' may denote hearth and home, pictures of Cinderella shivering by the ashes of the fire tend to accompany 'stepfamily'."[1]

These negative cultural stereotypes tend to make stepmothers—and stepchildren—the objects of prejudice. Marilyn Coleman and Lawrence Ganong from the University of Missouri at Columbia point out that "... though the stereotype of the 'wicked stepmother' may be more widely known, it is the term 'stepchild' that is consistently used to represent a negative experience or situation.... "[2] The term "stepchild" is used to describe someone that is marginalized, forgotten, or even victimized. One sportswriter for a leading American newspaper made the comment that so-and-so "was beaten like a stepchild."[3] Thus the image is perpetuated at all levels of society.

Our culture has made a stereotypical villain of the stepmother and a victim of the stepchild. The day when these destructive stereotypes can be tolerated is over. They are oppressive to stepfamilies. I heartily agree with stepmother Karen Savage when she urges that these images must be replaced by one of "resourceful, valiant women taking on the building of a new and growing family unit in our society. In spite of the cultural changes over the past few decades, mothers are still of primary importance in the family structure, and by the sheer number of stepfamilies being formed (almost 1,300 a day) it is a fact that stepmothers play a pivotal role in contemporary society."[4]

One new Christian stepmother told me she had never felt very good about being called a stepmother. Though she still doesn't like the negative images the term evokes, her feelings about *being* a stepmother changed one Christmas season when it dawned on her that Jesus was raised by a stepparent! God chose Joseph and entrusted him with the care of his only Son. Jesus grew up in Nazareth and the townsfolk called him "the carpenter's son." Surely, God did not place his Son in a "dysfunctional family," today's popular term for an emotionally abnormal family, but understood that step-parenting can provide a child with physical, intellectual, emotional, and spiritual nurture.

What to call the stepmother in a family is a big issue. Because of the negative stereotype that follows from the legacy of the "wicked stepmother," most stepfamilies work to avoid this pejorative term. We talk about blended families, second families, combined families—anything but stepfamilies. This is a good idea if avoiding the term contributes to a healthier family image. Author Jesse Bernard wrote that because of the emotion-packed connotations of the "step" terms many people avoided them whenever possible, for they are, in effect, smear words.[5] That's pretty strong language!

I recently came across a list of terms people should avoid when talking about children and their families. On this list, under "offensive terminology" was the term "stepparent." The suggested alternative was "parent by marriage." For most people, step-terms are offensive and so they look for acceptable options to step-terms.

Anne, stepmother to a teen-age stepdaughter, stressed she didn't like the term "stepmother" at all. In fact, when her stepdaughter wanted to joke with Anne, she called Anne her "stepmonster." Anne found nothing attractive in the stepmother imagery and told me, "I am not a stepmother. I'm a friend." She delighted that her stepdaughter had decided to call her "Mom."

This raises a key point. Anne's stepdaughter chose the name. Family relationships are generally happier if the child decides what to call the stepmother, instead of being told. What children decide may change over time, as the relationship changes. Young children seem to prefer "Mom" or "Mother," while older children may choose a first name. Some traditional women may feel that using a first name suggests emotional distance or even disrespect, and for them it may be best to settle on a nickname of some sort. The name itself is not the essential ingredient to family happiness. What is most important is that everyone involved—father, stepmother, and children—feels okay about the name.

In my own family the older stepchildren called me by my first name, and this eased us into friendship relationships which were more realistic and comfortable. The younger children, Kay and David, deeply desired a mother figure and chose to call me "Mom." They called their biological mother "Mama," so calling me "Mom" did not diminish their memory of her, but still gave them the mother they clearly needed and wanted. David tells me that it "helped to be able to call you by a different name, while still being able to use a very emotional moniker."

Sometimes what we call each other represents a much deeper issue. Author Claire Berman writes that "position, acceptance, respect, and love may be reflected in the appellation the stepchild bestows upon his or her stepparent."[6] Anne clearly interpreted her stepdaughter's choice of "Mom" as an expression of love and acceptance. When Rick called me "Mom" on our first meeting, he was clearly expressing acceptance although he immediately and naturally began to call me "Beth." Sometimes it bothered my younger two stepchildren to hear their older brothers and sister use my first name. They wanted us all to be a "real" family and names were important to them. But as the new adult in the family, I understood the greater importance of the honesty reflected in the names that each child chose and valued that above everything else.

My family has avoided using the terms "stepmother," "stepchild," or "stepfamily." We know that those terms describe us legally, but we don't use them normally. This is not a case of denial, for we are keenly aware that we have a unique family history. One look at us and you can tell! However, we want our family relationships to be healthy and positive and don't choose to harm our family with the prejudice that follows stepfamily stereotypes. Kay insists, "I cannot refer to you as my stepmother since you are truly my mother in all respects, except biologically."

An adopted child is not encouraged to find a different name for his or her mother, yet we tend to put some sort of onus on stepchildren and stepfamilies. We should allow stepfamilies the same freedom we allow adoptive families to use familiar terms that do not emphasize their differences from other families!

Until I began the research for this book, I rarely described myself as a stepmother. When I recall how God brought me into this family, I almost always talk about the fact that I "inherited" five children. This is contrary to the imagery that children are just "dumped" on the stepmother as part of the package when she marries their father. The reality is that Rick, Sharon, Steve, Kayleen, and David were God's gifts to me! My inheritance! I inherited them at different ages and stages, with varying needs and personalities, but I am grateful for them all!

Our imagery of the "wicked stepmother" is all too vivid and destructive. We can counter this imagery with the thoughts of Steve and Tim, two stepsons I interviewed, ages twelve and nine. These boys sat down with their stepmother and made up a list of "Things a GOOD Stepmother Does." Read with care a dozen suggestions offered by these young, but wise, children:

1. She tries to feed her child food that he regularly likes with some new things along the way—not all at once. This makes the child feel like you are listening to him.
2. She spends time with the child and gives him lots of attention.
3. She reads to him.
4. She plays games with him.
5. She supervises what he does. She behaves like a parent, not like a friend or another kid.
6. She is funny, makes jokes, and laughs with her kids.

7. She tries to get to know their natural mother, treats her with respect, doesn't embarrass her, and doesn't try to take her place.
8. When she is with her friends, she still gives attention to her husband. (She doesn't leave him out of the conversation).
9. She is modest in front of her kids, and they are modest in front of her.
10. She kisses her kids, except in front of their friends. She also hugs them when they come home from school.
11. She builds family traditions with her kids (like heart-shaped chocolate chip cookies on Valentine's Day).
12. She's interested in things the child is interested in. Though kids like to spend time alone with their father sometimes, the stepmother should feel included too. (The only exception is if she doesn't *want* to do something like go motorcycle riding with them.)

What a fantastic list! This sounds like a pretty GOOD Stepmother to me!

# TWO

# Twenty-One and the Mother of Five!

*It is never simple—it is never "boy meets girl" but rather woman meets man, and man's children, and sometimes man's ex-wife, ex-in-laws.... It's a package deal.*

*The Good Stepmother: A Practical Guide*
**Karen Savage and Patricia Adams**

WHEN I DREAMED MY PRINCE would come on his shining white horse, I never envisioned five additional ponies escorting him to my side! Never once did I say to myself, "Someday when I grow up, I think I'll marry a thirty-eight-year-old widower with five children." But that's exactly what I did!

When I finished college in 1967, I was just twenty years old. Returning home to western New York State, I landed a summer job as an occupational therapist trainee at a state mental institution and then scouted the local school districts for a teaching job. With great excitement, and a good deal of trepidation, I secured my first position in education. I would teach Spanish in a nearby high school, junior high school, and the evening adult education program. My next task was to find a place to live.

Jan and Donna, two Christian girlfriends that I had known most of my life, approached me about possibly finding a place together. We scouted the local paper and found an ad for a little house that sounded just right! The ad described the rental as a "two bedroom bungalow, furnished, and reasonable." We needed at least two bedrooms, we owned almost no furniture, and very little else—including money, so "reasonable" was essential! The ad did not include an address, just a phone number.

We dialed the number, were given the address, and scheduled a time to look at the home. It was just what we needed—cozy, clean, furnished, and affordable! We took it. As we walked out the front door to our cars, Jan noticed the house across the street and commented that she thought that was Dr. Brown's house.

Dr. Brown had moved to Williamsville a few years before to assume a faculty position at the local state university. He and his family joined our church and became actively involved. One tragic day, Dr. Brown's wife fell ill around noontime and passed away that evening. The doctors determined that she died of a cerebral hemorrhage. This left Dr. Brown, a widower, with the full responsibility for raising his five children.

As Jan, Donna, and I settled into our new home, we discussed the possibility that God had placed us in that very house so that we might be able to minister to the four children across the street. (Rick, the oldest, had left to attend school in Oregon). I played the guitar, and sometimes Sharon, Steve, Kayleen, or David would come over just to sing along, have some popcorn, or just talk. During our first few weeks in the new home, we enjoyed getting to know the kids. On several occasions, we visited in their home as well.

In the absence of a mother, the Brown house was showing need for a little care. While Dr. Brown took his children on a canoeing trip that August, my roommates and I entered his house, cleaned it top to bottom, gathered dirty clothes, laundered and mended them. The family was happily surprised and pleased to find a clean house when they returned home from their vacation.

Early that fall, Dr. Brown needed a date for a faculty dinner at the university. He was not particularly anxious to date again, as he continued to deal with his loss, keep things running at home, and handle his professional responsibilities. But his colleagues pressed him to bring someone, threatening him if he showed up alone. Taking the coward's way out, he asked his older daughter, Sharon, if she would go with him. Sharon responded just the way any seventeen-year-old with a life of her own would, "No way, Dad!" The children, however, eager to help their Dad out of a fix, discussed the matter among themselves, weighed the alternatives, and voted that their father should ask me to be his date! They came to him *en masse* with their suggestion.

So Dr. Brown came over one evening, told me about his need to take a date to this faculty function, about Sharon's refusal, about the kids' vote as to who his date should be, and about my victory! I was both amused and pleased with the children's vote of confidence! I would have been willing to help him out, but I had already promised to do something else.

In my mind, we were not really discussing a "date." This is important to understand. I was just twenty years old, and someone thirty-eight seemed very "old" to me. (This is no longer true now that I'm in my forties!) I referred to Dr. Brown as "Dr. Brown" and placed him in the category of "friend of my parents."

One Friday evening that fall, my parents dropped over to visit me. Dr. Brown called the three of us over across the street to take a look at his brand-new Chrysler. He offered to take us all for a ride, but Mom and Dad needed to get home and didn't have the time. Dr. Brown turned to me and said he really needed to get supper for the children, but then he'd love to take me for a spin. I said, "Sure."

Fresh out of college, beginning teachers, and trying to pay back college loans, my roommates and I were poor. Stretching our meager budgets, we used to eat a lot of pasta. When I went back to my house that Friday night, I ate a large spaghetti dinner with Jan and Donna. Then I freshened up, just in time for Dr. Brown to arrive at my door to take me for the promised ride in his new Chrysler.

We drove along for a few minutes with my saying nice, rather surface things like, "This sure is a great car!" (What did I know about cars?) Then Dr. Brown turned to me and said, "You know… it's been a long time since I had a quiet dinner out and away from my children. Would you mind if I bought you dinner?"

This came as a surprise to me. I didn't have plans for the evening, but I thought this was going to be just a short ride together. He seemed so sincere in his invitation. I didn't know him well enough to be honest and admit that I had just finished a sizeable spaghetti dinner less than half an hour before our ride. So, I said, "Sure, that would be very nice."

We drove out of town to the Apple Grove Inn where the *maitre d'* seated us at a beautiful table for two, right next to a center, circular fireplace. Despite my large "appetizer" of spaghetti, I savored a steak that night, complete with baked potato, salad, and even dessert!

That's not all that I savored! Dr. Brown and I sat and talked for the four most enjoyable hours that I could remember in a long time! I saw that he was not only very kind and very bright, but that he was committed to the same basic values in life I cherished. He clearly had a love for God, a deep relationship with Jesus Christ, and a desire to please God as a person, father, and professional. We enjoyed the time together immensely and the evening was over before we knew it. He drove me home and I was happy, and *full*!

It wasn't until after he left me at the door and I was back inside my own house, I realized what was happening to me: I was beginning to care for a thirty-eight-year-old man with five children! But it was too late, I was hooked. I had dated a great deal in high school and in college, but I had never enjoyed and admired anyone as much as I enjoyed being with Dr. Brown that evening. I thought he was terrific! It seemed apparent that the feeling was mutual because he made a point of seeing me the next day and told me he couldn't remember enjoying an evening more.

We both wanted to spend more time with each other, and we did, as much as we could around our busy fall teaching schedules. We fell in love quickly. The dumbest thing I have ever said in my life, I said the night that Don first told me he loved me. We were on a short date together after a Sunday evening service. He turned to me and said very tenderly, "You know, Beth, I really love you." Then I said—yes, I really said this—"I love you too, Dr. Brown!" We fell in love so fast that one of my hardest tasks was to shift from "Dr. Brown" to "Don." Now Don laughs and calls that the moment when I showed him the greatest respect!

When a woman comes into the life of a man who is a single father, they become friends, then better friends, and then the man decides that it is time to introduce her to his children. These introductions can be awkward for both the woman and the children. A potential stepparent must court the children as well as the future spouse. It has been said that first marriages break up because of the couple; second marriages end because of the children.[1]

I am grateful that God brought me into the lives of the children first. In fact, they sincerely and legitimately felt that they found me for their father. After all, they were the ones that decided I would make a good date for him. In some sense, Don was not saying to them, as typically happens, "Here's your new mother and I hope you'll learn to love her!" They had found me, we were friends first, and then I learned to love their father. That made the beginning of my relationship with my family much easier.

However it would be dishonest to say that our courtship

was easy. We faced a great deal of criticism, and even rejection, from various family members, and from some church friends. It was painful for all of us. When a woman takes on five children, concern is normal, and when she is only twenty-one, there is legitimate cause for worry. As a very young, single woman, I would be making enormous changes in my life. Marrying a father is different from marrying a single man. I lacked experience both in being married and in raising children. Major adjustments were ahead of me.

The concern was easier to accept than the rejection. Still, through the months of courtship, Don and I were both convinced of our love for each other and our shared commitment to build a new family with the children—a family that would bring honor to Christ. We were further convinced that God would provide the strength and wisdom required.

I was not the only one stepping into a challenge; Don was risking too. He was taking on a young wife. He wanted me to be happy, to feel accepted by the family, and to find fulfillment as a person. We moved ahead, against the odds, because we were confident that God was present in our lives and would provide for us.

I'm convinced that deciding to marry again is even harder when the stepfamily is born out of divorce. After weighing the circumstances of their unique situation, couples contemplating a second marriage should turn to God, as author Paul Cullen suggests, who will enable them to move ahead: "Faith in God stabilizes the couple's relationship and allows a person to say 'I do' again, to be open and vulnerable to another again, to seek intimacy again, to create memories of family life again, to see God through the love of another. Through prayer, God gives understanding and hope in situations that seem desperate."[2]

Happily, after we had been married for a while, concern for my adjustment waned, criticism diminished, and most of the relationships that suffered during our courtship were fully restored. God's faithfulness had sustained us.

I can still remember the day when Don called all the children together in the living room and announced that he and I were going to get married. There was general excitement and happiness. We'll never forget the honest response of Don's fifteen-year-old son, Steve, who looked at the engagement ring and then at his Dad, asking, "And how much did that ring set us back?" We still laugh about that.

Children deserve time to get used to this potential newcomer in the family long before their father makes any announcements. They need to have time to get to know their father's friend and discuss any feelings they have about her. When their father decides to remarry, they should not be shocked by the news. They should see the second marriage as the natural result of their father's growing love for the new woman in his life.

However, when the father announces to his children that he will marry again, it should be just that—an announcement. Cherie Burns observes that: "A father who gives his child veto power over his choice of mate does everyone a disservice. He undermines the authority of both adults, not to mention his own happiness, should his child rule against his choice. In addition, he wrongs the child by allowing him or her to take responsibility for adult relations."[3]

Tell your children, don't ask. Each couple needs to decide how this would be best handled. It may be best to tell the children first when they are alone with their father so that they can discuss any questions or feelings that they have about the decision. If the pre-engagement period has been happy and accepting, perhaps the future stepmother could share in the moment.

Don and I planned our wedding to take place during Christmas vacation. We had a small church wedding and then a marvelous, but brief, three-day honeymoon in Toronto.

If I have a regret about that time, it's that we planned our wedding quickly and did not fully involve our children in the ceremony. Still our daughter, Kay, has more encouraging memories. She recalls "I was very excited about the upcoming wedding, and although I don't remember 'helping' to plan anything, I never felt left out. I knew what the flowers were going to be, the colors, and who was doing what. I think that I was treated as someone important throughout, at least that's how I felt."

These feelings of belonging are the most valuable part of a celebration and I am happy for Kay's memories. David's favorite memory of the wedding day is a moment we shared during the wedding reception: "You walked over to me and said, 'Hi, Son!' I responded with an enthusiastic 'Hi, Mom!' And we hugged. It's funny how a moment like that can cement a relationship."

When a biological mother is expecting her new baby, friends give showers, family members send gifts, women who are already mothers share abundant advice, everyone takes pictures, and there is an air of celebration over the pregnancy and the birth. But when a woman becomes Mom No. 2, there are no showers, no gifts given to the children, no advice shared on how to be a good stepmother, and no pictures taken. I sincerely believe that the inclusion of a ritual to celebrate the new stepmother/stepchild relationship would be beneficial to everyone.

Possibly this moment of celebration could be part of the wedding ceremony. Several stepmothers that I have interviewed included their stepchildren in the wedding ceremony as maids of honor, ushers, or ringbearers. One stepmother mentioned that the pastor offered a prayer of thanksgiving for her stepchildren during the ceremony, and he prayed for them individually and for their relationship with their new stepmother.

For other couples, it might be best to find a private moment before or after the wedding to celebrate as a family. The father and stepmother should reassure the children of their love for each other and their commitment to the children. It might add to the long-term impact of the occasion if the parents gave special gifts to the children as a lasting token of their commitment.

In our family, the first celebration ritual was my first Mother's Day with the children. They gave me Mother's Day cards and conspired together with their Dad to buy me a "mother's ring." I'll never forget how happy I was to receive that ring as a token of my new relationship with the children. Five stones were mounted on a wide gold band. I wore that ring with great pride and affection.

When Don and I returned home from the honeymoon, we moved the remainder of my few belongings across the street to his home, which was now ours. At age twenty-one, I was Mrs. Brown and the mother of five children: David, age 9; Kayleen, age 10; Steve, age 15; Sharon, age 17; and Rick, age 18. Life would never be the same!

# THREE

# Born of Loss

*All changes, wished for or not, involve loss... For step-family members, the changes that they experience are more in number and of much greater magnitude than typically occur in the early years of first marriage families... a step-family is a family born of loss.*

**Old Loyalties, New Ties**
**Emily B. and John S. Visher**

STEPFAMILIES ARE NOT NEW. They have been part of our culture for a very long time. In colonial America, the nuclear family was not the norm. Complex family structures with stepmothers and stepfathers abounded. The high mortality rate due to difficult childbirth, disease, and hard work led to numerous second and third marriages. So great was the concern for stepchildren, that special courts were created to oversee their welfare. "The stepparent was considered a replacement parent, someone who 'stepped in' to rescue the bereaved family."[1] The term "step" always denotes loss, deriving its meaning from an old English word meaning "bereaved" or "deprived."

Stepfamilies today are even likelier to occur following a divorce, which makes the current context of the stepfamily more complicated than ever. Today, for every stepfamily formed through the death of a biological parent, six are formed through divorce.

The roots of stepfamilies are different from nuclear, first marriage families. Pretending that they are just the same as any other family is detrimental to their healing and growth. It is *critical* to remember that *stepfamilies are born of loss*.

The loss of the first wife and mother in a family has a powerful effect on the stepmother, her husband, and her stepchildren. In seeking to build a healthy family unit in the present, the stepmother must be realistic about the pain of loss in her family's past. Paul Cullen warns that "Guilt, anger, and decimated self-esteem resulting from divorce or the death of the first spouse also contribute to the major struggles in second marriages. Because these emotions haven't been adequately dealt with, they reappear as unwelcome guests in second marriages."[2] This means that stepmothers cannot close their eyes to negative emotions and unresolved loss, but must face them and actively enter into the healing process.

Stepfamily experts debate whether the stepmother who replaces a deceased parent encounters more difficulty than the stepmother who replaces a living parent. Early researchers believed that becoming a stepmother through death was more difficult.[3] When death claims the natural mother, she is often idealized by her grief-stricken husband and children. In their mourning, the family is quick to forget her faults and eager to remember her strengths. A stepmother sometimes feels like she is competing with a saintly ghost and destined to lose. She will never measure up to such an ideal! Children in bereaved stepfamilies are usually older than children in divorced families, and older children tend to have greater problems in accepting a stepmother. These stepmothers typically come into the family after the children and their father have experienced an extended time as a one-parent family, finding roles solidified and family members less open to change.

Other stepfamily experts, while acknowledging the obstacles to stepmothering bereaved children, insist that it is more difficult to be the stepmother following a divorce. This is because the biological mother remains on the scene, an ever-present, and often competing, influence on the children.[4] She is usually awarded sole or joint custody of the children, giving her perpetual prominence in the lives of her children. Even if the biological mother does not live near the stepfamily, nor share in the custody of the children, nor keep in contact with her children, her influence is inescapable. In the past she has powerfully shaped family values, beliefs, and attitudes and will always be a force in the stepfamily's present and future.

Whether a woman becomes Mom No. 2 through death or divorce, she faces considerable challenges. Her family is very different from a nuclear family in its relationships. Jeffry Larson, comments that, despite the great differences in their origins, "... stepfamilies are often treated as nuclear families by society and in most cases, not understood."[5] A stepmother helps her stepchildren by honestly trying to understand them. She begins by admitting to their loss.


## STEPMOTHERING FOLLOWING DEATH

Peter, a young pastor in his early thirties, stopped by my seminary office for a chat. He knew that I was researching a book on stepmothering and he wanted to talk to me about his stepfamily. When Peter was just six and his younger brother only four, their mother died. The father remarried a young woman who took on the task of raising them. Peter talked about his stepmother with great love and admiration. He had vivid memories of her sacrificial love and care. But, Peter also had a point to make. "Be sure," he told me, "that you tell stepmothers not to act as though the first mother never existed." He went on to describe how, after the second marriage, pictures of his first mother disappeared from the house and she was seldom discussed. The boys felt her loss deeply but were not given the freedom to remember her and grieve her absence. Today, as young adults, these sons still struggle with unresolved feelings of loss.

A stepmother, whose stepchildren are now adults, confided in me that her family did not discuss the deceased mother much. She now regrets this, telling me, "I wish I'd known how important it was to talk about her." Her stepsons, teenagers at the time of her marriage, never talked about their feelings for their first mother and now, as grown men, they wish they had. They, too, keep bumping up against their feelings of unresolved grief.

David Mills reports that "a significant number of children (8.5 percent) lose one parent through death during their childhood. It is likely that very little can match the devastating effect of a parental death on a child."[6] He also notes that men do not tend to wait as long as women to remarry. In those families it is unlikely that the children have had as great a time to recover from their loss by the time the father remarries.[7]

Mills describes the typical bereaved stepfamily as "... one where the father and stepmother are happily in love with each other, and the children are overwhelmed with ambivalent emotions and feel misunderstood or somewhat abandoned by their father."[8] Stepmothers who enter the lives of children whose mother has died, enter their lives at a time of great pain and conflict. Their mother's death may cause the children to feel abandoned, helpless, frightened, or even hostile.

Though it may be easier on a new marriage not to endure conflicts with an ex-wife, bereaved stepfamilies may be harder on the children than divorced stepfamilies. These children "experience a greater sense of loss and conflicting loyalties than they would if their mother were living. They worry that their father's new marriage negates their mother, and even suggests that perhaps she was never loved. So they often vow to remain loyal, to tend her flame. Obviously, a stepmother in these situations is going to have difficulty."[9]

The bereaved father and his children remember the deceased wife and mother and, in many cases, exaggerate her noble qualities and forget her weaknesses. She becomes, in their memory, a wife and mother that would outshine any other. When Mom No. 2 enters the picture and inherits the legacy of Mom No. 1, she may feel defeated before she ever begins. According to psychiatrist Willem Bosma, "Where a child continues to mourn a dead parent, the child's fantasy may have built the parent into something beyond the realm of comparison, and over the years, whenever a problem comes along, the child will blame the stepparent because the dead parent—who is close to perfection—could certainly never be at fault.[10]

## MAKING FRIENDS WITH MEMORIES

What can Mom No. 2 do to help her children grieve their loss and more easily accept her into their family? Her first responsibility is not to live in a world of denial herself. She is not the first mother on the scene. The children have a Mom No. 1 whom they loved and whom they miss. They have a right to their memories of her and need to talk about her. Instead of being threatened by those memories, stepmothers should encourage the children to recall those memories and to discuss their feelings. This way, Mom No. 2 is not coming between the children and their loyalty to their first mother. The stepmother reduces the conflict in their minds by allowing them to love and cherish their Mom No. 1, while growing in their love for their Mom No. 2. As a stepmother, I sincerely thank God for my children's first mother. If it was not for her, I would not have these children in my life now.

In my early years of stepmothering, I was so young and overwhelmed with personal adjustments that I did not pay enough attention to the adjustments of the children. I assumed their grieving process was over when I married their father, and I only learned in later years that it was not.

Our comfort is in knowing that our God is a gracious God and he can bring healing into our lives and into the lives of our children at any age or stage. If you are a stepmother and believe that your children are still grieving their mother's death, become a patient, and caring listener. Galatians 6:2 offers a command and a promise: "Carry each other's burdens, and in this way you will fulfill the law of Christ." The law of Christ is love (Rom 13, Jn 15). When we carry the burdens of our stepchildren by giving them the time and the freedom to grieve, we are expressing our love for them. We love them by listening to them. If your stepchildren are uncomfortable about confiding in you, find them a trustworthy, mature Christian in whom they can confide.

## DON'T COMPETE WITH MOM NO. 1

Children may very well exaggerate the accomplishments of their first mother. This is normal. The need to idealize her and the need to talk about her should lessen with time and maturity. In the meantime, stepmothers would do well to resist any temptation to compete, and to keep their sense of humor. Cynthia Lewis-Steere offers some excellent advice when she says, "No matter how many of your new stepchildren point out that they never ever saw a fallen chocolate cake like yours in their lives, don't be discouraged. That memory may or may not be true. Keep your sense of humor active and laugh with them at your cake."[11]

Besides encouraging the children to remember and not competing with their memory, stepmothers should be sure that the children can hold on to memorabilia as well. Eric McCollum tells of a stepmother who "made sure her stepdaughters had a chance to take some of their mother's belongings for keepsakes. This effort signaled that she wasn't trying to replace their mother and that she respected their need to remember her. The girls chose some china and toys and felt better about their father's new wife."[12]

Good stepmothering in bereaved families does not mean that you diminish your role as the present wife, or as Mom No. 2. Love means setting limits, for older stepchildren as well as for younger ones.

When Trish married Bob, he had several grown children. In the intervening years between the death of Bob's first wife and his marriage to Trish, Bob and his children grew very close. When Trish came into Bob's life, these children had difficulty relinquishing their father's attention. Instead of being happy that their father now had a wife with whom to share his life, they exhibited signs of jealousy and resentment. They continually referred to Trish's home as their mother's home and developed a pattern of talking about their mother and excluding Trish from these conversations. Worried about the effect her feelings might have on her husband and grown stepchildren, Trish decided to bury her hurt and not make an issue of it. But that proved to be ineffective and even destructive. Feelings of alienation and anger only deepened and caused her increasing pain.

Trish gradually learned to accept the memories the stepchildren had for their first mother, but she also learned to be more assertive about her new relationship with their father. She developed more confidence in her role as Bob's wife. She asked Bob for help in making her feel more included in family conversations. Trish and the children are still working out the boundaries and privileges of their distinct relationships with Bob. These adjustments can be difficult for everyone, but they are worth the time and effort they require.

There are no easy answers to offer families when they grieve over the death of a mother. But our God of mercy is gracious and full of compassion (Ps 111:4) and he can bring healing to the husband and children. It is possible that he may use the stepmother as his chosen agent in this process.

My son David recently shared with me his memories of the awful night when he lost his mom: "I remember the night that Mama died. Kay was lying in her bed. I was lying down on the floor next to her. We heard sirens, some tense talking, some crying. Kay and I just listened. Finally Kay said, 'Mama's dead.' I answered, 'Not yet.'" David adds, "Though I very much wanted Mama to live, when she died God gave me a real strength and calmness to pass through the difficult times. When I began to develop a relationship with you, I began to draw on more security from you."

If Mom No. 2 cooperates with God, praying *for* the children, praying *with* the children; listening to their memories, their questions, and their hurts; and if she gives them—and herself—time to heal from the effects of the loss that gave birth to this new family, she may see God use her in her family's healing. What a privilege!

## STEPMOTHERING FOLLOWING DIVORCE

When I was a little girl growing up in a Baptist church, divorce was a rare event. I knew of only one lady in our church who was divorced and she was often referred to as "Mrs. So-in-So, who is divorced,"—all in one breath. Attitudes toward marriage and divorce are vastly different today, even within the church, than they were twenty or thirty years ago. Pressures on today's families touch everyone. As David and Bonnie Juroe observe, Christian families can no longer continue to say, "'It can't happen to us.' It can and is happening with great regularity just as in nonChristian families."[13] The sad reality of divorce in the local church is undeniable.

Of course, every woman considering marriage to a divorced father should examine the Biblical teachings on divorce, but it is not my purpose to discuss those issues or make a judgment on them here. Given today's reality of divorce and remarriage, I would like to offer hope and instruction to those who have married and become stepmothers to their husband's children.

In Malachi 2:16 the Lord says, "I hate divorce." Anyone who has experienced divorce can understand why a compassionate God would decry an act that tears people apart and creates so much pain. Divorce creates feelings of failure, anger, loss, and mourning. After divorce, we use terms like "broken homes" or "failed marriages." Divorce is rarely a clean break. Adults who divorce need time to heal. They must learn to let go of the previous relationship, to seek forgiveness, and to forgive their former partner. This process of divorce recovery usually takes between one and five years. Only when the formerly married person has truly let go of the past, is he or she ready to start over.

Divorce involves a terrible loss and it takes time before a healthy, new marriage can begin. Sadly, many a parent remarries without adequately mourning the loss of a shattered marriage.[14] When this is the case, issues of blame, anger, pain, and bitterness can emerge in the subsequent marriage. The Vishers also observed that the divorced parent may enter this second marriage with an unfulfilled need for affirmation from the ex-spouse:

> Whether or not the remarried parent was the one who wanted the divorce, the wish for affirmation can remain, although it tends to occur more frequently for the one who has been actively rejected. The person who did not seek the divorce keeps hoping that the former spouse will say, "I really do think you are a very nice person, even though I wasn't able to stay married to you." The one who chose to leave the previous marriage hopes to hear, "I really do think you are a good person, and I understand that you needed to leave."[15]

Divorced stepfamilies are born of loss. Divorce often means the loss of unity in the home, the loss of former extended family relationships, the loss of both emotional and economic security, and the loss of self-esteem. As a woman decides whether to marry a man who is a divorced father, she needs to determine if this father and his children have experienced a process of divorce recovery. If they have not, she will be stepping into an emotionally and spiritually needy family, and her presence may make matters worse. When families take time to heal *before* Mom No. 2 comes into the picture, the climate of the fledgling stepfamily is much healthier.

Recently, Karen married Gary, a divorced father of one young son named Shawn. Though the love that Karen and Gary feel for each other is genuine, their marriage is off to a rough start, because Gary has brought to the marriage many feelings of guilt and anger. He never sought help in dealing with his sense of failure in his first marriage, and he feels particularly guilty over "abandoning" Shawn, who now lives with his natural mother. Shawn only visits Gary and Karen for short periods of time, and Gary wants to spend every minute with Shawn alone. Karen, who like most stepmothers can see her stepson only during his scheduled occasional visits, feels shut out of Gary and Shawn's relationship. Wisely, this couple is seeking counseling. Again, at whatever stage, God can do a work of healing. Gary needs to deal with his feelings of failure from the past marriage, build a new sense of oneness with Karen, and determine what would make Shawn's visits the most beneficial for all three members of this stepfamily.

Knowing the losses experienced by families broken by divorce, a stepmother can again be God's servant in the process of healing. The family must give itself time to adjust and ready itself for a fresh start in the second marriage, and it must deal with residual feelings of loss.

## BUILDING ON THE FUTURE

One of the myths of stepmothering is that a stepmother can compensate for the loss in the family. Stepmothers may "attempt to be overly warm and loving and give a lot to the stepchildren. Problems can arise from this when the husbands begin to feel deprived or left out. The stepchildren may view this extra attention as an attempt to replace their natural mothers. It is not possible to take away or make up for past pain."[16] A stepmother cannot undo the divorce. She cannot replace the first mother. Her presence today does not mean that yesterday's pain is gone.

Though stepmothers cannot erase the pain of the past, they can be proactive in minimizing the pain of the future. They can work to *build family unity*—to foster mutual decision-making in a supportive environment. They can *encourage the continuation of relationships among extended family members*. Grandparents, aunts, and uncles usually want to continue to be part of the children's lives. Stepmothers and fathers should also *foster a climate of emotional security*. One stepmother, who had been married three years, told me that her two stepchildren got so upset when she kidded about a make-believe fight with their father, that she quickly learned not to kid in that way. These children were frightened at the thought of more parental conflict. This stepmother learned that her husband and her stepchildren need to hear words of love, appreciation and encouragement from her. The family needs to know that she is glad to be part of them and is committed to their well-being.

## "GO IN PEACE" OR YOU'LL GO TO PIECES!

Stepmothers, like all Christians, are called to be peace-makers. This can be a pretty tough assignment, and is ultimately impossible apart from the power of God in our lives. How is it possible to be a peacemaker in a family born of divorce?

First, we need to find our peace with God, before he can do his powerful ministry through our lives. Romans 5:1 reads, "Therefore, since we have been justified through faith, we have peace with God through our Lord Jesus Christ." By faith, we must receive God's great gift of love and forgiveness by acknowledging our sin and inadequacy and by receiving Christ's great sacrifice for us when he died on the cross for our sins. When we find our peace with God, he fills us with his Spirit. And it is the Spirit of God that empowers us to be peacemakers (Rom 8:6). After we experience peace with God and receive the power of the Holy Spirit, then it becomes our responsibility to draw on that power as peacemakers. Romans 12:18 tells us that, if it is possible, as far as it depends on us, we should live at peace with everyone.

One of the stepmother's central tasks, in stepfamilies born of divorce, is to make peace with her husband's ex-wife. Only those who are in this circumstance fully understand what a challenge this can be!

Ruth sat across the table from me, sipping a cold lemonade. I was struck by her warm eyes framed by an unusually soft, clear complexion. I somehow expected her voice to be gentle and I was not disappointed. But when we talked about her husband Mike's ex-wife, Susan, Ruth spoke honestly of a difficult struggle. She readily confessed, "I was angry and bitter toward Susan because she made the children feel guilty for the pain that she felt about the divorce... I really prayed about my relationship with her. I wanted to do what's right and I prayed that the Lord would help me to want to forgive her." Then she underlined the fact that she hadn't prayed about *forgiving* Susan. She began by praying that she would *want* to forgive Susan. Ruth understood a fundamental truth. She could not love Mike's ex-wife in her own strength. She did not even want to love her. So Ruth prayed that the power of God would work through her, changing her, and enabling her to love the children's first mother. God answered her prayer. She was, in God's power, able to forgive Susan. Ruth even encouraged the children to write and sustain a relationship with their first mother.

Carrie, stepmother to two children, wisely concluded that "the important thing to remember is that you share in common an interest in the well-being of the children." That's what stepmothers and ex-wives should agree on—what will be best for the children. Many stepmothers in families born of divorce stressed the importance of treating the ex-wife with respect. They found early in their role as Mom No. 2 that putting down Mom No. 1 only harmed the children. Stepmothers should not worry that the children's love for their natural mother will in any way diminish their love for their stepmother. Jamie Keshet puts it this way:

> Love does not come in measured doses. The love we give one person does not take away from the love we have to give others. Help the children see that you really want them to have a good relationship with their absent parent.... A good relationship with an absent biological parent helps the child to feel good about himself. In the long run, your stepchild will thank you for your efforts. Stand in the way of that relationship and someday he will curse you for it.[17]

Anne told me that she has no relationship with her husband's ex-wife. "She hates me. She blames me for the divorce and I didn't even know her husband back then." Though the children's first mother was bitter and estranged from her children, Anne understood the strength of the bond between her stepdaughters and their natural mother. Anne could show love because of God's love. She helped her stepdaughters to "keep the door open" with their natural mother. She reminded them to send cards and gifts on

Mother's Day and on their first mother's birthday. She was a peacemaker in God's name.

A stepmother's role as peacemaker also extends into the lives of her stepchildren, who may be smothering in confusion and bitterness. The loss experienced by children in divorced families is notably different from that of the adults. David and Bonnie Juroe note that children suffer from a loss of *identity:* "A child's identity lies with both of the natural parents. When one goes, a part of him goes. The biological parents provide for children a sense of *who* and *what* they are. Therefore, when there is a separation, it represents a loss of love. The feelings of rejection can be most serious."[18]

As children of divorce grapple with their sense of identity, they discover that their task after divorce is the opposite of their parents' task. The parents are separating, drawing away from each other, finding stability, and trying to start over. The children, on the other hand, want to hold on to a relationship with both their mother and father. They still want and need these relationships which are so central to their identity. Parental reassurance at the time of divorce and during divorce recovery can abate the children's identity conflicts. Parents need to explain that though they are not living together any more, they both still love the children very much and will continue to be a strong part of their lives. Children need to know that the divorce was not their fault, but the result of parental conflict and failures.

When Mom No. 2 enters the lives of children of divorce, the picture may darken for the children, at least initially. Their worst fears have come to pass, as all hope for their natural parents to reunite is dashed. A relative stranger is now occupying their father's attention. Familiar family structures are gone. Perhaps there are other children in the family now. Where once the child might have been the oldest, he or she may now be displaced by an older stepchild. The child who was the baby of the family may have lost that status to a stepmother's younger children. These changes can make a child feel very vulnerable and fearful. "Divorce can shatter a child's concept of permanence and respect for relationships, especially if the child believes that he or she is no longer part of a close-knit family unit."[19]

The stepchild's loss may be expressed in a variety of ways. The child may become antisocial, throwing tantrums, starting fights, or crying. The child may lose interest in school, resulting in lower grades. Some children may withdraw from the stepparent and the natural parents. They fear emotional involvement.

This distancing can be unnerving for Mom No. 2 who longs for a growing relationship with the children. Some children try to cope with their loss privately, without showing emotion. Even when a child appears to be coping with loss, the father and stepmother should not assume everything is okay and that there is no need for intervention. Whether or not children of divorce express their pain, they feel enormous loss and are deserving of Mom No. 2's attention and care.

## HOW TO HELP

How can Mom No. 2 help these children who have suffered the loss of divorce?

1) Try to get the children to talk about their feelings over the divorce and their feelings about the present family structure. Enroll them in divorce recovery workshops for children if possible.

2) Listen without being judgmental. Criticism is a sure way to lose their confidence.

3) Work to restore the child's self-esteem. Children of divorce have many misgivings about their own value. One way to help children feel better about themselves is to give

them responsibilities in the home. When they fulfill those responsibilities, offer the child honest praise for a job well done.

4) Discipline the children when needed. Involve the children in determining the rules for your family. Make sure that they clearly understand your expectations and then enforce the rules fairly, but firmly. This is another way to reassure children that you love and value them.

5) Avoid needless conflict and handle disagreements gently, being sure that everyone feels free to share their feelings. If you have a disagreement with your husband, work it out when the children are not present. If you argue in front of the children, they will exaggerate your conflict and worry about whether your marriage is going to make it.

6) Pray with and for your children. Thank God for them. Pray for their healing. Pray for their future.

All change involves loss, but change can bring gain as well. Change can mean a new beginning, a time of new growth, new challenges, and new happiness. Stepfamilies are born of physical death or the death of a marriage, but they symbolize a commitment to continued life. Stepfamilies want to go on living, learning, and loving.

# FOUR

# Love Me Tender, Love Me Now

*It may take several years for a stepfamily to become a unit. To expect instant love is to set the stage for personal hurt and disappointment.*

**Step Families: the Growing Majority**
**Paul Cullen**

MARIA RUSHED DOWN the heavily treed path, swinging her guitar case and valise, and singing enthusiastically to boost her confidence. She was overwhelmed by the thought of her anticipated new responsibilities as a governess to the seven children of a widowed former naval captain. As she neared the captain's estate, she sang with exuberance: "Let them bring on all their problems. I'll do better than my best. I have confidence they'll put me to the test, but I'll make them see I have confidence in me!" As Maria finally arrived at the gate, her eyes widened with apprehension and she whispered, "Oh, help!" But, despite her fears, she stepped forward to take on the challenges of the captain and his children with all the courage she could muster.

As I watch the *Sound of Music*, I am charmed by the story and the music, but I am utterly amazed at the speed with which Maria endears herself to those children! Only fourteen minutes after Maria introduced herself to seven ill-mannered, blatantly resentful children, they began to arrive in her room to find comfort during a ferocious thunderstorm. After some hugs, comforting words, and a song about her favorite things, Maria had won their affection! The very next day (only seven more minutes into the movie), the whole tribe was off for a picnic in the Alps—running, laughing, and singing together!

The real Maria Von Trapp probably took much longer than a day to earn the love and trust of her charges. The real world and the world of spectacular media productions are often far apart!

Our media-driven culture of quick fixes, simple solutions, and instant love, sets us up for sure disillusionment and disappointment when we bring those expectations into the reality of stepfamily life. And yet, this myth of "instant love" prevails. New stepmothers gaze hopefully at their stepchildren, thinking "love me tender, love me now!"

This expectation of instant love is most common among young stepmothers who step into the lives of children whose mother has died. After the wedding, as this new bride turns her attention to the children, she may discover that it is harder to love the children than she anticipated. She may even discover feelings of resentment towards the children when they do not respond positively to her. All of this leads to feelings of failure and guilt.

When Dad and the future Mom No. 2 are dating, their feelings and the children's feelings are often at opposite extremes. The adults are caught up in their discovery of one another—their new sense of love, commitment, and hope. They are dreaming dreams of their wedding, their honeymoon, and their future life together. The children, however, may be unhappy and confused. This new marriage signals the end to their dreams. It means that Dad and Mom No. 1 will never be together again. It means that Dad will have less time for them, and perhaps less affection. Children, who have been hurt once already, may be unduly cautious or perhaps jealous. Children are also fearful. They know their father, but they don't know the new stepmother very well. They don't know how she will react to them when they fail. They don't know her moods, her rules, her expectations.

As Dad and the prospective Mom No. 2 plan their new life together, they typically envision a brief time of adjustment and then the birth of a happy family. This rarely happens. And when it doesn't happen, they are likely to feel overwhelmed by feelings of inadequacy and failure. Mom No. 2 may ask herself, "What's wrong with me? Why can't I love these children? What's wrong with them? Why can't they love me?" These questions not only breed guilt feelings in Mom No. 2, they may also feed a growing resentment which she harbors toward the children.

## RULE NUMBER ONE

The number one rule for new stepmothers is: *Give yourself time to adjust!* You are stepping into a brand-new family with many unknowns. You are going to need time, and lots of it, to begin to understand your husband, your stepchildren, and your own place in the family.

Laura uses the word "strained" to describe her first years as stepmother to two teenage boys. Because Laura never had children of her own, and because she grew up with sisters and no brothers, she didn't have a clue about how to raise boys. She remembers those early years as "scary for both sides."

Laura discovered early on that she could not step in as a "mother." The boys did not want that from her and clearly rejected her attempts to be a parent. If she said anything to correct their behavior, they usually wouldn't say much in response, but they would give her hostile and critical looks, and continue doing just what they had been doing. Sometimes they would fling an angry retort and their blatant disrespect hurt Laura significantly. She remembers one occasion when her stepson answered the telephone. He told Laura that the phone call was for her but she didn't hear him. So he yelled, "What's the matter with you? Are you deaf?" Laura felt very ashamed and embarrassed as she picked up the phone to talk to her friend.

Overcoming her stepsons' resentment was important to Laura, but not easily managed. She made a firm decision to show an interest in these boys and began by attending all their sports events. Both stepsons were very athletic and were extensively involved in their school's athletic programs. Laura attended all of their games even if her husband had to work and it meant going by herself. Since one of her stepsons was in junior high and too young to drive, Laura often drove him and many of his friends to the games.

Laura also preserved and encouraged the family's practice of attending church together. She understood the value of Christian training and worship and she also understood the value of being together as a family in worship. Her commitment to family togetherness included extended family members as well. She worked to develop close ties with extended family, making sure that her stepsons did not feel cut off from their maternal grandparents. Even though Laura was the newcomer to the family, she joined in the traditional holiday celebrations at her stepsons' grandparents.

These conscientious attempts to affirm her stepsons and to express her genuine commitment to them did not go unnoticed. The boys were eventually won over by Laura's consistent concern for them. After several years, her stepsons grew to respect her and to value Laura as the good friend she had proven herself to be. Laura gave herself time to learn how to befriend her stepchildren and her efforts, *over time*, paid off.

## RULE NUMBER TWO

The number two rule for stepmothers is: *Give the children time to adjust!* Not only are our expectations for ourselves too high, they are too high for the children. Author Ralph Ranieri offers some good advice: "Keep your expectations of the child at a minimum. Start with respect. If your stepchild treats you with respect, then relax. Respect is fundamental. Once you have this, many other good things will flow into the relationship if you give yourself and your children time to make adjustments."[1]

Most parents in stepfamilies expect the children to become immediately and deeply involved in the newly formed family. Limit these expectations too. It's sometimes a surprise to find that older children may have special difficulty in quickly committing themselves to the new family because they may feel that their involvement may be in conflict with their loyalty to the old family. Children, not unlike Mom No. 2, may need time to develop a sense of intimacy and comfort in the stepfamily. If the child withdraws, becomes moody, or acts out his or her fears, it's easy for Mom No. 2 to blame herself. But it is likely, even probable, that it isn't her fault, and blaming herself only creates additional guilt that the family can well do without. Instead of blaming herself, Mom No. 2 can give the child her respect and give the child time to sort through feelings and conflicts that still haunt him or her. Give the child time!

My daughter Kay confesses, "I do remember, at times, feeling left out of the special relationship that you and Dad shared. I remember shortly after you and Dad were married, Dad left me alone in the living room to go talk with you. I remember thinking to myself, 'he is *choosing* to spend time with Mom instead of me.' That was a pretty devastating thought to a known Daddy's girl. I didn't resent you, but I do remember being a little hurt by Dad's defection. I also remember thinking it was supposed to be this way, and that I would have to get used to it. I guess I did." Kay understood her own need for time to adjust.

Time allows us to get to know one another. As Cherie Burns wrote, "Stepmothers and stepchildren have a relationship a lot like partners in an arranged marriage."[2] They live in the intimacy of a family setting and yet are barely acquaintances.

When Don and I were first dating, I asked him all kinds of questions about the children. I knew the children a little from spending previous time with them, but Don had known them all their lives. He patiently answered my frequent queries, telling me what the children were like when they were small, what they liked to talk about, how they liked to spend their free time, their strengths, their struggles. This was helpful in several ways. After we were married, this kept me from giving myself too much credit for their strengths or blaming myself too much for their struggles. Knowing more about them made it easier and more natural to establish a warm relationship with them.

Of course, the best way for Mom No. 2 to know the children is to spend time with them herself, especially time talking together in relaxed settings. During my first months of marriage, I learned so much about my oldest stepdaughter, Sharon, while we shopped together for her college clothes and supplies. In a recent phone conversation (some twenty-three years later), Sharon reminded me of those first shopping sprees. She loved being with someone close to her in age. "You showed me that being a teenager could be fun," she said.

Steve, on the other hand, was only fifteen—an understandably awkward age to have a twenty-one-year-old mother. He spent very little time with me or with the rest of the family. I was hurt that he always chose to be with his friends rather than with family. I've learned since that his behavior was typical of many adolescents. Steve needed the freedom to establish relationships in the family at his own pace and in his own way.

Kay and David liked to run errands with me. A treat at the village donut shop or ice cream store gave us time alone to talk. We got acquainted at a relaxed pace, and with no hidden agendas. Kay now tells me, "You spent a great deal more time with me than I was used to getting from an adult. I remember that you played board games with me, talked with me, made me feel free to bring friends home to visit, decorated the dining room up special for my birthday—all the things a little girl of ten or eleven who had been the fourth of five children never remembered receiving. In some ways, I became the oldest child and I loved every minute of the new attention and privilege."

## STAGES OF THE STEPFAMILY CYCLE

Ranieri warns us to avoid the "as if" tendency: "A blended family cannot be expected to operate as if it were a nuclear family. This is an unrealistic expectation which denies the unique strengths and ignores the inherent problems of the blended family."[3] Mom No. 2 will be less stressed, confused, and guilt-ridden about feelings of jealousy and rejection, if she understands the ways in which stepfamilies are different from nuclear families and if she understands the rather predictable stages of a stepfamily's development.

Educator Patricia Papernow describes seven stages of the stepfamily cycle:

1) *Fantasy:* This is the stage where the myth of instant love prevails. The stepmother fantasizes about how her love for the stepchildren will compensate for their previous loss. The children fantasize about how things used to be.

2) *Assimilation:* The stepmother attempts to live out her

fantasy, but instead feels confused and disappointed. She may experience some feelings of jealousy, hostility, and resentment. She wants to be part of the biological parent-child unit, but often feels left out. She may feel rejected by the children but not know what to do about it.

3) *Awareness:* This is a time of honest appraisal. The stepmother now recognizes some of her feelings for what they are, admitting her disappointment in the children and in herself. She admits that she is inadequate to live out her fantasy. At this stage, a stepmother may seek help in understanding her stepfamily—from a friend or a book about stepfamilies. Or the family may move to a new home where there is a sense of a new start. These changes lead to the next stage.

4) *Mobilization:* The stepmother becomes more assertive, sharing her honest feelings and needs. Some stepmothers receive support from their husbands and stepchildren which helps them to deal with their feelings and get their needs met. But for most, the mobilization stage is a time of conflict. When the stepmother shares her feelings, other family members do too. Family members may polarize over the issues that arise in this stage.

5) *Action:* Now the father and stepmother work together to define their roles and relationships. Consideration is given to the ways in which the biological family unit has done things in the past, as well as the stepmother's needs and ways of doing things. Couples learn to spend time together to listen to each other empathically and to work out a course of action for their family. Stepmothers now begin to form relationships with the children independent of their father's involvement.

6) *Contact:* This is the time when the stepmother and her husband draw very close to each other. They begin to experience a deeper level of intimacy because they are living authentically. They are sharing feelings and working out their relationship honestly. The stepmother is experi-

encing deeper levels of intimacy with the children as well. At this stage, the stepmother has finally and clearly defined her role in the family.

7) *Resolution:* By the final stage, the marriage relationship has become stable and strong. A new family history is underway and family functions have become routine. The stepchildren are valued yet released to form their own identities.

Papernow discovered that it takes four years for "fast" families to move through these stages; seven years for "average" families; and more time for other families.[4] Most remarried parents call it quits on their marriage after three years—before the stepfamily has had sufficient time to get in synch. They fail to realize that becoming a functional stepfamily takes time. The process cannot be rushed—there are too many changes taking place!

If you are experiencing alienation, conflict, and discouragement in your family now, work to identify the causes of those feelings and begin to share them with your husband. You can overcome your feelings of failure and guilt by facing the issues squarely and learning to discuss them with your husband in an honest and loving way. Realize that you are in a process that takes several years or more. Work patiently to understand yourself and your new family.

## LEARNING TO LOVE

The fantasized ideal of love in the stepfamily where the stepchildren and their stepmother are mutually devoted is seldom achieved. And even when warm and loving relationships develop within a stepfamily, stepmothers struggle with their belief that they should love all their children in exactly the same way. This unfounded belief sets up Mom No. 2 for unnecessary and painful feelings of guilt. As Cherie

Burns writes: "It's unwise for a stepmother to expect or pretend that her stepchildren will be like her own children, no matter how close the relationship between them might be."[5] Karen Savage, stepmother and author, describes a stepmother's different loves: "In real stepfamily life, this duality of mothers is a reality. Stepmothers and stepchildren have not experienced a primal bond, and their relationship starts out at a more complex level.... The relationship between mother and stepchild is not fixed instantly like the relationship between mother and newborn infant. It is a relationship that evolves over time—and it will be different than the biological bond."[6] Admitting these differences ought to bring great comfort to Mom No. 2. She should not expect to love all of her children in the same way. When she enters the lives of her stepchildren, she has missed the moment of normal bonding that mothers experience at the birth of their natural child.

Though Mom No. 2 may not love her stepchildren spontaneously, "Christian love does not have to be spontaneous to be genuine."[7] In life, we usually need to *work* at establishing relationships. Spontaneity takes a back seat to the consistent and persistent Christian love that every stepfamily needs.

The absence of primal bonding does not mean that we cannot come to love our stepchildren deeply and genuinely. It does mean that stepmothers must, as David Mills describes, "'artificially' re-create a period of time for nurturing without limit-setting, to allow for bonding appropriate to the age of the child."[8] This bonding period can take about two years. The absence of primal bonding does not mean that a stepmother cannot love her stepchildren. It simply means that she loves her stepchildren *differently* from her biological ones. As stepmothers, we can learn to respect, nurture, care for, discipline, pray for, and enjoy our stepchildren. Though learning to love your stepchildren takes time, the end result is well worth it! One stepmother wrote, "It occurs to me that the pain associated with developing a blended family is not unlike that of childbirth. It is really worth the pain when you view the outcome!"[9]

Ruth became stepmother to two preschool boys. She tells them now, "You didn't grow in my womb; you grew in my heart." That says it!

The age of the children will make a difference in the bonding experience. Most experts agree that it takes preschool children less time and effort to adjust to stepmothers than older children. Adolescents have the toughest time of all. The reality is that children will accept your love in varying degrees. Some will form strong bonds with you, others will accept your friendship only, and others may reject your love entirely. It depends on children's bonding patterns with their natural mother, their age at the time of your marriage to their father, and their own temperament.

I remember an early bonding moment with my new daughter, Kay. Our similarity in appearance gave Kay and me an uncanny family resemblance. We both had fair skin, blue eyes, and light brown hair. This added to people's confusion about our relationship when we were together. Not many months after Don and I were married, Kay and I went to the hardware store together. We found what we were looking for and headed to the cashier stand to pay for it. The cashier overheard Kay call me "Mom." She stopped and looked at me saying, "My! You look so young for this to be your daughter!" I looked at Kay and she looked back at me as a wide smile spread across her little girl face. Kay offered no explanation to the cashier so neither did I. I simply said, "Thank you." I looked at Kay with eyes of deepening love. She was obviously pleased that the lady thought I was her mother. Kay was saying by her silence that she wanted me as her mother and, at that moment, I began to *feel* like her mother!

David was only nine when I married his father. We warmed to each other easily, but I especially remember our bonding moments as we attended church together. As we filed into our usual church pew, David always made sure that he sat next to me. He'd cuddle up close to me. Though he was small then, he used to reach up high and put his arm around my shoulder, or he would hold my hand as we sat through the service. He was clearly happy to have me in his life. I never held David as a little baby, but I felt his touch as a little boy.

Love is a decision for both Mom No. 2 and her children. It cannot be forced. A stepmother is not the savior of the family. Her role is important, but limited. She cannot solve all the family problems by herself. Knowing this, she should relax and allow the children to relax too. That way, everyone can work together to get to know each other and figure out their part in each other's lives. If you want to give your stepchild a special gift, let the child set the pace. Don't rush love. Let it grow patiently. Given sufficient time, most children are able to form a close relationship with their Mom No. 2.

"Instant love," like instant anything, is a poor substitute for the real item. Like cheesecake, love is sweeter and richer when it's patiently made from scratch!

# FIVE

# Candlelight, Kisses, and Kids: Early Adjustments in the Stepfamily

*The lack of privacy quickly becomes an issue with all couples where children are present at the start of marriage and even more so by first marrieds who are unaccustomed to the pervasiveness, and the ongoing nature of the presence of children.*

*Making it as a Stepparent: New Roles/New Rules*
**Claire Berman**

D ON AND I WERE MARRIED in a little country church on the Thursday afternoon following Christmas. We left that same day amid showers of rice and well wishes for our honeymoon in Toronto, Canada. Sunday, just three days later, we returned home. Monday, we unpacked our luggage and celebrated New Years with the children. Tuesday, we headed back to work. The children returned to school, Don left for the University, and I resumed my role as a high school teacher. When the last school bell rang that Tuesday afternoon, I did not head home to unwind, but to prepare dinner for my new husband and four of his children. My life had changed suddenly and dramatically in just a few days.

I arrived home, changed clothes, and took a quick survey of the tiny kitchen. I didn't know where anything was kept, except for a few of our wedding gifts which I had placed on the kitchen counter. I looked through the refrigerator, making little sense of its contents. The dinner hour loomed large before me and I was beginning to panic. Finally, I made a quick grocery list and headed for the store. I bought what I needed, returned home later than I had planned, solicited the help of the kids in setting the table, and somehow prepared a simple meal. The meal disappeared quickly, nobody died from my novice cuisine, and I felt a strong sense of accomplishment. After dinner, Don helped me wash the dirty dishes and put the kitchen in some kind of order. Dinner was over. I was exhausted.

Those first few weeks of marriage involved more adjustment than I had ever made in my life. I was no longer single, but married. I had children to care for. I was in a strange house. And I was a first year teacher, keeping just a few days ahead of my students in my lesson preparations. I was completely overwhelmed.

That was half of my lifetime ago. I look back at those early days now and think, "Of course, I was overwhelmed! What young bride wouldn't be!" But back then, I was so sure that I could "do it all," that I became very discouraged when I found that I couldn't. I couldn't keep up with the tasks of managing a household, let alone finding enough time to get to know my new husband and children. I loved Don, I was glad I had married him, but I was exhausted and disheartened at the mountain of new responsibilities. One author describes these circumstances well: "A woman with no children of her own, when involved with a man with children whom she wishes to marry, may entertain unrealistic fantasies about how wonderful life will be with him and his children.... After marriage, and the lessening of romantic euphoria... the bride may become oppressed with the new burden she has taken on. Other women ease into the role of motherhood and gradually become accustomed to its frustrations. Having it thrust upon her cannot but produce feelings of being trapped and overwhelmed."[1]

Clearly, I needed to make some changes. Just two months after my wedding, I decided that I wanted to quit my teaching job and give full-time attention to the family. Don supported my decision. Quitting meant less income and a delay in my career plans, but I would gladly trade my modest paycheck for a modest amount of sanity! The school principal found a replacement teacher six weeks later, and I left teaching to become a full-time wife and stepmother. This was a wise move. Being freed from the pressures of my job gave me time to adjust to the many demands of my new life.

Once I admitted my inability to handle a new job, a new marriage, and new children, I felt a great sense of relief. I was not disappointed about leaving teaching. Instead, I felt challenged by the new role I was playing in my family. I could focus both time and energy on developing my relationship with Don and the children.

## ELUSIVE PRIVACY

Becoming a bride and a stepmother calls for many adjustments beyond the demands of a first marriage family. In most first marriages, a couple can count on at least a year alone—getting to know each other and easing into married life. In a stepfamily, there is very limited privacy and time as a couple from the first day. Stepfamilies are born of loss. Either through death or divorce, fathers and children lose the family unit they experienced with the first mother. Sometimes we forget that stepmothers experience loss too. They lose their girlhood dreams of married life—of romantic dinners and quiet evenings with their new husbands. They lose privacy.

Our first Saturday at home, Don and I slept in late and lingered in bed, relishing the intimacies of our newly married life. Wrapped in each other's arms, our marital bliss was interrupted by a loud banging on the bedroom door. "What do you want?" asked Don. "Dad, when are you going to get up?" said a young voice. "Pretty soon," answered my beloved. A few minutes later, a second bang rattled our bedroom door. "Dad," asked another voice, "is it okay if we have some ice cream?" "Not this early in the day," said my beloved. The mood was broken. Don and I got up and dressed. This is the reality of newlywed life in a stepfamily, where privacy is elusive, but not impossible.

I paid thirty dollars for a table for two. Thirty dollars. A good chunk of our monthly household budget but a crucial investment. I remember that little table fondly because it became a symbol to me of marital romance in the midst of sometimes chaotic family activity. The table was very simple and very small, with a formica top and chrome legs. I placed it under the kitchen window, justifying its purchase because I desperately needed more workspace in my tiny kitchen. But that little table was much more than extra workspace. That table became a romantic rendezvous with my new husband.

One night a week, Don worked later than usual, teaching an early evening class. The children didn't want to wait until eight o'clock to eat their dinner, so I fed them, and afterward they disappeared to do their homework, watch TV, or spend time with their friends. After cleaning up the kitchen, I set my little table for two, prepared a special dinner for two, located some soft music on the kitchen radio, and lit two candles. I remember the first time that Don arrived home to find this scene! He was so surprised! He laughed his big laugh, gave me a hug and kiss, and joined me at the little chrome table for two. We spent a couple of hours lingering over our meal together. We discovered a small moment, one evening a week, to be a couple. In the midst of a household of kids, we made time for kisses and candlelight!

## ELUSIVE ACCEPTANCE

New stepmothers are typically overwhelmed at the numerous adjustments they face when first married. Not only do they deal with a constant lack of privacy, they must also adjust to a greatly increased workload in caring for an entire family. Besides learning to cook for six or seven people, I faced a mysteriously sinister and continuously growing mound of dirty clothes. I used to say that my laundry basket reminded me of the famed "widow's cruse of oil" (1 Kings 17:16). No matter how much wash I did, the basket was always full!

Beyond adjusting to minimal privacy, and increased work, Mom No. 2 must also adjust to the presence of children in her day-to-day life. Most stepmothers do not have custody of the children full-time and this gives them time in between visits to catch their breath, and ready themselves for the next visit. But many stepmothers, including the one-sixth that entered the family following Mom No. 1's death, have the children all of the time. In either case, the children quickly become Mom No. 2's greatest challenge.

Most stepmothers crave their stepchildren's acceptance. As they enter the marriage, they find that this acceptance is not a given, but must be earned. Stepparents June and William Noble write: "You have no biological ties to the children; you are there solely because you happen to marry... their parent. Any respect, any deference you get will probably have to be earned; nothing comes to you by virtue of position within the family. *In many ways you will have to prove yourself to become accepted.*"[2] (Emphasis mine.) This need to "prove yourself" can become increasingly stressful for a new stepmother. She moves cautiously in her relationship with the children, hoping to please them, hoping to win their respect, trying to be sure that she is exact and fair. In this regard, stepmothers are much less spontaneous than natural mothers. And the children are less spontaneous in their relationship with her:

> One stepdaughter... likened the caution of a step relationship to an in-law one: "You react spontaneously to a parent," she explained, "and no matter how angry you become or how intemperate your speech, most of what is said in anger is forgotten. In dealing with a stepparent, you are conscious of your tone and your testimony.... You're always aware of the relationship."[3]

While it is true that stepmothers must earn their children's respect, trust, and love, unrealistic standards of success can defeat stepmothers from the start. The reality is that every mother, step or natural, blows it. Every mother disappoints her children on occasion; every mother becomes impatient; every mother sometimes deals unfairly with her children. Every mother makes mistakes. No new stepmother will ever be a perfect mother! A stepmother cannot win the children's love and acceptance by her perfection, but by her authentic acceptance of the children and of herself.

Self-acceptance means that you receive the unconditional love God has for you. Fortified by his love, you can recognize that your own worth is not measured by your *performance* in any role, including your role as a stepmother. Your worth rests in your *relationship* with God as God's child!

Self-acceptance means that you give yourself a break. It means that you recognize that you are a "vessel of clay" as it says in 2 Corinthians 4:7. God's Spirit is within you, but you are human. Self-acceptance means that you recognize your weaknesses, ask forgiveness when you fail, and move ahead with your life. When you are a stepmother, you will make mistakes with your children. When you treat them unfairly or become impatient, apologize and move on. But don't write yourself off as a failure! And when you make mistakes, accept God's forgiveness and then forgive yourself.

I remember, in my early days as a bride, rushing through the grocery store looking for an easy dinner! I came across a plump little chicken, smeared with barbecue sauce, that looked pretty delicious. I rushed home and threw that bird into the oven for one hour at 325 degrees. I thought I'd let it roast while I put the groceries away and fixed the rest of the meal. Not many minutes later, black smoke began pouring out of the oven and blanketing the house. I didn't know that when you bought barbecued chicken that it meant the bird was already cooked! I choked, teared up (from smoke and embarrassment) and then began to laugh! We removed the charred, crisp, black chicken from the oven, opened the windows, aired out the house, and let the Kentucky Colonel save the day! My inexperience in the kitchen was plain to see: I was no gourmet cook. But the only healthy thing to do was to learn from my mistake, not take myself too seriously, and keep growing. I think this is a plan worth remembering for all stepmothers.

Laura would agree with me. She remembers one stressful day when she lost her temper. The family was moving from one home to another and everyone was tired and on edge. Laura's teenage stepsons were helping out some but, in her estimation, they were not doing enough. Her frustration grew during the day until, finally, she let loud, angry words fly. Her stepsons yelled back. They all said hurtful, irretrievable things to each other.

Laura felt terrible and overcome with guilt. "I knew that their mother [who had died] would never have said such things," she lamented. Laura's relationship with her stepsons was very tense and fragile and no one wanted to talk about their verbal battle.

What did Laura do? She prayed and she asked God to forgive her and to help her. She determined to learn from her own mistakes and to work for peace in her home, not dissention. She worked to control her tongue "and," she says, "I gave myself time." Gradually, Laura did gain better control of her tongue, and the conflicts with her stepsons lessened.

The process of acceptance may begin with accepting ourselves as we are, but it also means accepting the children as they are. When you enter the lives of these children, you must accept them, not for what you will make of them in the future, but for who they are now. Acceptance does not rest on the children's behavior or attitudes toward you. The apostle Paul reminded us that God's love reached down to us while we were yet sinners. Christ died for sinners, not saints (Rom 5:12). Later, Paul reminded us that we should "accept one another, just as Christ also accepted us to the glory of God" (Rom 15:7). So we are to *accept* the children, no matter how they feel about us. Acceptance does not mean that we condone their behavior or enjoy their rejection. Acceptance means giving these children encouragement and emotional support no matter what. Acceptance means we love our new children with no strings attached. We love them in Jesus' name.

## FRUSTRATED AND FRIGHTENED CHILDREN

In the early stages of a stepfamily, stepmothers are not the only ones learning to adjust; children are faced with enormous changes as well. One popular myth about children in new stepfamilies is that children adapt easily to the new situation. This is simply not the case. Researchers Wallerstein and Kelly, who studied the children of divorce, found that, "even at the five-year point, one-third of all children were still being seriously affected by the divorce (as manifested by serious depression, poor school performance, and behavior problems), and that another third were still being affected, but less seriously."⁴

For the first few months, the stepfamily may be in a honeymoon phase since the children appear to accept the changes occurring in the household and offer little complaint. But this phase is usually followed by a stormy period when their pent-up frustrations are vented with great emotion.

The frustrations of stepchildren are understandable. They feel that they have very little power in the family, very little control over the changes around them. They might have been included in the discussion about their father's upcoming marriage, they might have had a part in the wedding, but they actually had little say about the marriage. They may be living in a different house, going to a different school, or adjusting to other children living in their household. They often feel helpless to stop the roller coaster of change which they are riding.

These changes are threatening. They create fear; fear of being out of control, fear of the future. The early stages of remarriage require learning to love frightened children whose world has been turned upside down and whose foundations of security have been badly shaken.

Mike and Susan divorced when their sons, Jed and Norris, were one and two years old. Mike received custody of the boys. Ruth married Mike four years later. Ruth became Jed's mother when he was only five years old, and she came to love him quickly and unreservedly. Because Jed was so young, and because Ruth so often assured him of her love, Ruth assumed he was secure in her love. She was shocked to learn from Jed many years later that it was not until junior high that he finally believed that Ruth would stay. Having been rejected by his first mother, he worried for years that his second mother might leave him too.

In the early stages of stepfamily life, the children's fears may appear as rejection of the stepmother. They may feel there is too much risk in loving another mother figure. They may reject the new mother's attempts at building a relationship. The toughest test of all may be at the beginning of the stepmother's newly married life. The children may test the strength of her commitment to the family. She must demonstrate through her behaviors, attitudes, and words that she is in the family for the long haul.

Sometimes the most difficult adjustment is for the oldest daughter in the family. After a divorce and, more often, after the death of the first mother, the oldest daughter is often called upon to assume some domestic responsibilities and much of the care for the younger children in the family. Her status shifts from child to a "surrogate spouse" to her father and a "surrogate mother" to her younger siblings. Depending on the personality of the daughter, the circumstances of the mother's absence, and the length of time before the remarriage, the adjustment for the oldest daughter to the new stepmother can be very difficult. Having functioned temporarily as an authority figure in the family, she may struggle to accept someone else in that role.

Some daughters, on the other hand, welcome Mom No. 2 as a release from adult responsibilities they assumed of necessity, but not by desire. Don's oldest daughter, Sharon, was sixteen when her mother died and seventeen when I came into her life. During the time when there was no wife or mother in the home, her status changed. Her Dad confided in her more and relied on her help more than ever. Sharon could have resented my intrusion into the family but she did not. Instead, she felt relieved, making my transition into the mother role easier than it might be for most stepmothers. Sharon was concerned about the welfare of Kay and David, the youngest two in the family, and she was happy that someone was now in their lives to take care of them. She did not want the responsibilities of caring for a home and family.

She wanted to be a teenager and she wanted to get on with her own life. Recently, she tried to describe our relationship by saying, "We have a special closeness that God has given us. The Lord gave us to each other." Thankfully she saw me as God's provision for our family. Many daughters would not. We need to understand the struggle of these daughters whose identity and security are threatened when they are asked to relinquish important roles to a new stepmother.

In addition to negotiating a relationship with Mom No. 2, some stepchildren face the enormous challenge of adjusting to stepbrothers and stepsisters. If both parents bring children to the marriage, the number of new relationships in the family becomes increasingly complex.

Happily the friendships between children have a good chance for success. Researcher Lucile Duberman found that 62 percent of the stepfamilies she interviewed rated the relationships between stepsiblings as either "excellent" or "good." She also learned that relationships between two sets of children fared better when they all lived in one house, rather than in two houses, and were even happier after the remarried couple had had a child together. This adjustment to stepbrothers and stepsisters also had a greater chance for success when the father's oldest child was less than thirteen years old.[5]

## THE POWER OF POSITIVE COMMUNICATION

During the early phases of adjustment in your stepfamily, empathize with your stepchildren, showing that you understand the loss, the pain, and the stress of their many adjustments. Don't assume responsibility for the children's behaviors or attitudes, which were well-developed before your marriage, but try to understand them.

Understanding comes through communication. Communicate your care and concern for the children and your desire to know them better. Be sure your husband communicates that his love for them has not changed now that he loves you. The children need to hear that your presence does not mean he has less love for them. Be sure that communication is honest and open. Don't let the children play one parent against the other. Talk with the children together with your husband and let them know that you both are committed to their well-being. Family meetings can be very helpful in the early stages of stepfamily life. Let the children ask questions, vent their frustrations, and express their worries. Demand respect, but do not require agreement. Let the children talk about their real feelings. It will be easier to deal with the problems in your new family if you know what they are. Cutting off a child's negative emotions will leave you in the dark and the problems will worsen.

Try to find time with the children one-on-one. I wish that I could have had more time with the children individually when they were small. Our family was so large and so busy that I did not have much time to sit with just one child at a time and explore how things were going. This is something I appreciate about the stage of life I am now enjoying. I love being free to focus on my children one at a time!

Right from the start of your marriage, work to establish cordial relationships with members of the extended family. Many stepfamily experts agree that much stepfamily dysfunction comes from outside the stepfamily unit; from a former wife, or former in-laws, or other members of the extended family. This increases the temptation to avoid these relationships, cutting them out of the new family structure. But a loss of these relationships can be disconcerting to the children, only adding to their sense of loss. Loving inclusion of the extended family can only work in Mom No. 2's favor, as well as in favor of her new family, making the children feel more secure.

During your first days as Mom No. 2, listen to the words of stepmother Cherie Burns:

Stepchildren warm to a stepmother slowly. Because they have witnessed the disintegration of their parents' marriage, they want to avoid experiencing a sense of loss again. They withhold affection, even from persons they may be drawn to and like, until they sense and see that the new person's presence is permanent and worth their effort.... A stepmother should convey a sense of confidence and positivism to her stepchildren instead of seeming to wait for their approval.[6]

This means that as we begin our lives as stepmothers, we should not be governed by the attitudes of our stepchildren. We are only responsible for our own attitudes. The tone that we set for the family will, eventually, make an enormous difference in the adjustment of every family member.

What attitudes should we bring to our new role as stepmother? Paul gives some excellent advice to the Philippian church (Phil 4:8) and I would like to personalize it for us as follows:

Finally, stepmothers, whatever is true, whatever is noble, whatever is right, whatever is pure, whatever is lovely, whatever is admirable—if anything is excellent or praiseworthy—think about such things.

What in this new family is true? is noble? is right? is pure? is lovely? is admirable? What in this family is excellent and worthy of praise? Think right now about your own stepfamily. What good family qualities come to mind? Don't keep these treasures a secret; let your family know the good things you have discovered about them. It will encourage them!

Rather than mourning your lack of newlywed privacy,

think about the fine husband God has provided in your life. Rather than rehearsing all your mistakes, learn from them and thank God for the things that you are doing well. Rather than dwelling on the children's rejection of you, praise God for this chance to love some grieving children. Think about the admirable qualities of your husband and children and concentrate on them. Finally, don't keep your "attitude of gratitude" a secret. Let the family know that you are happy to be a part of their lives.

Paul completes his advice with a powerful promise. If we put these positive attitudes into practice, the peace of God will be with us (Phil 4:9). The pain and struggles of early adjustments in stepfamily life will not disappear, but we will face the challenges strengthened with God's peace.

# SIX

# Mom No. 2 Is a Married Woman

*The bonds of matrimony are worthless unless the interest is kept up.*

—**Anonymous**

ONE EVENING, AFTER I HAD SPOKEN about Christian parenting in a church service, Karla worked her way down to the front of the sanctuary to talk with me. She introduced herself and said how much she had enjoyed hearing the story about my marriage and experiences as a stepmother, but she wanted me to know that her story didn't share my happy ending.

Karla had married a divorced father of five young children. After willingly giving many years to the care of his home and his children, this stepmother proudly watched all of her stepchildren grow into fine young adults and leave home to live on their own. Just after her youngest stepchild left, Karla's husband announced that the marriage was over and that he had found someone else. Karla was devastated. She concluded that her husband had only married her to provide for the needs of his children, and not because he loved her. She may have been right. What amazed me about our conversation, were her words of gratitude and deep affection for the children in spite of her husband's cruel rejection. "I've been so terribly hurt by my ex-husband," she said, "but I am so happy to have known and loved his children!" I admired Karla very much.

Loving her husband's children is one convincing way for Mom No. 2 to show her love for her new husband, but it isn't everything. A woman needs to love and be loved as a wife apart from her role as stepmother. In all the demands of being Mom No. 2, she can easily lose sight of her primary relationship as a wife. Mom No. 2 is a married woman.

## THE SECOND TIME AROUND

The lyrics of the old popular tune proclaim that "love is lovelier the second time around," but it's not necessarily so. In the last couple of decades, while the divorce rate climbed to over fifty percent, the redivorce rate after second marriages climbed as well, so that the odds of a second marriage failing are now between fifty-five and sixty percent. Americans have one of the highest divorce rates in the world, yet they continue to remarry after divorce, hoping for marital success the second time around. The statistics tell us that they probably won't find it.

Why are second marriages prone to fail at a higher rate than first marriages? It could be that the issues that caused the breakdown of the first marriage were never resolved and were simply carried over into the second marriage—issues like unrealistic expectations for the marriage, lack of communication, financial problems, alcoholism, addictions, or infidelity. When these problems begin to surface in the second marriage and are added to the pile of adjustments unique to a stepfamily, hope for a happy marriage dies easily and the marriage disintegrates. Stepmothers Elizabeth Einstein and Linda Albert write that "one of the greatest fears of people in stepfamilies is that of another failure. If this marriage seems to be a replay of your first one, your commitment to the stepfamily may be weak.... Some people, knowing they can survive the pain, might again consider divorce as the solution."[1]

Second marriages often encounter enormous stress. Not only do couples face the adjustments that first marriage newlyweds have in learning to live with each other, but they must also adjust to the personalities and demands of a ready-made family of children. In addition, these couples usually have added financial pressures and, in stepfamilies of divorce, legal entanglements from the first marriage. And finally, they often must cope with the hurt and unhappy relatives of the former spouse.

Second marriages seem plagued by an overload of guilt. Mom No. 2 and her husband may bring guilt over a failed first marriage into their new marriage. Parents who remarry often feel guilty about loving their new spouse, feeling somehow that their marital love is a betrayal to the children who have been a part of their lives for a longer period of time. In a first marriage this is clearly never a problem.

A failed second marriage would only magnify Mom No. 2's feelings of guilt and disillusionment, raising a question as to whether or not a second marriage is worth the risk. Is there any hope for happiness?

## ADVANTAGES OF A SECOND MARRIAGE

The losses and regrets from a first marriage may sabotage any chance of happiness in a second marriage but, surprisingly, they also may enhance it. A good second marriage may mean more to those who have known the pain of a difficult first marriage. Joan's first marriage to an alcoholic was very difficult and became abusive emotionally and physically. Now, though she has the added responsibilities of stepchildren, she is married to a kind and supportive Christian husband. After telling me her stresses as Mom No. 2 she ended our conversation with an exuberant declaration, announcing, "I love being married to my husband!" The added responsibilities are worth it to Joan who now knows what it means to be loved by a caring husband. No longer abused, she feels cherished.

Though second marriages have added pressures, they also have some distinct advantages over first marriages. Some of the unrealistic expectations brought to first marriages vanish. Couples now realize that some tough adjustments are ahead and that they will have to work at making their marriage a good one. Mom No. 2 is apt to discard the Cinderella dream of marrying her Prince and riding off into the sunset happily ever after. She more likely envisions a warm and satisfying companionship with her new husband, as they learn to accept each other, to respect each other, to enjoy each other, and to love each other. She knows this relationship won't just naturally fall into place but will require hard work and unfailing commitment if the marriage is to last.

Typically, couples in second marriages are older and wiser and perhaps less likely to repeat the foolish mistakes of their youth. Learning from their mistakes, they may be more patient with each other and more tolerant of each other's weaknesses.

Greater maturity often means that these couples are more established in their careers which can further ease the pressures in their home. When I married Don, he was thirty-eight years old. He had completed his formal education and was established as a professor in a state university. Though his work was demanding, he was far less pressured than in his earlier days when, though a husband and father, he worked a full-time job while attending graduate school. Don's professional stability contributed to the emotional, as well as financial, security of our family.

During his time as a widower, Don worked hard at caring for his children while keeping up with his career responsibilities. Those demanding days gave him a profound appreciation for the hard work of home management and child care that men who have not functioned as a single parent may never understand. Don's enhanced sensitivity to the demands of keeping a home functional and happy enriched our life together from the very first day. Often husbands in second marriages are less likely to take their wives for granted.

## MAKING MARRIAGE WORK

Not many years ago, two researchers interviewed happily remarried couples to discover what made second marriages work. What were the keys to happiness the second time around? They found three answers to this question. Happy second marriages were characterized by: 1) good communication; 2) minimal conflict; and 3) shared decision-making.[2]

### Good Communication

When Joyce and Matt married they blended two families—four children from Joyce's first marriage and three from Matt's. Some of their kids were pretty "mixed up," according to Joyce, and were struggling with drug addiction and emotional problems. Life with these children was not easy, but Joyce and Matt survived by developing good communication skills.

"We are extremely honest," says Joyce, even though this is sometimes painful for her. Joyce had been afraid to be honest in her first marriage to an alcoholic husband. In that marriage, honesty sometimes earned her verbal abuse. But Joyce has discovered that she can trust Matt to listen to her with love and without retaliation. They decided together not to let problems get by, but to discuss them openly and honestly. "We spend a lot of time talking," Joyce continues. "We know each other's needs and we care about them."

Joyce and Matt have discovered the stability that comes from talking together about problems. They have learned to listen to each other—to listen with open minds and hearts so that they can help each other deal with problems.

Mom No. 2 should tell her husband about her fears, and listen to his. She should discuss her needs, and listen to his. She should clarify her family goals, and listen to his. She should share her insights about the children, and listen to his. She should identify problems that she encounters in the family, and let her husband do the same. Trying to hide fears and avoid problems only harms the couple. As author Cherie Burns warns, "Good sportsmanship works against them if it obscures their willingness to recognize complex problems and work together toward solutions."[3] Honest communication allows Mom No. 2 and her husband to identify problems and work for their solution together. This builds trust between them, causing their love to grow.

We all grew tired of being told how "quality time" somehow compensated for minimal "quantity time" spent with our children. Not surprisingly, child development experts eventually rethought this notion and decided that both quality and quantity were important. We must give our children focused attention, and lots of it, if we want to be nurturing parents. The same is true in our married lives as Mom No. 2. We must give our husbands "quality time" and lots of it!

The secret to a happy stepfamily is a happy marriage. I repeat. The secret to a happy stepfamily is a happy marriage! As stepmothers Elizabeth Einstein and Linda Albert emphasize:

It is critical that you understand the importance of *making your couple relationship a priority*. If you do not nourish your marriage, you may not stay together. A major reason for divorce among remarried couples is that the wife and husband *fail to spend enough time* working to build their relationship. With the focus immediately and constantly on the children and their needs, the marriage never has a chance to take root and grow.... Even if your marriage does not end, *your stepfamily cannot stabilize until your couple relationship does.* Until children feel that your marriage relationship is solid, they may remain withdrawn from stepparents, afraid to trust.[4] [emphases mine]

Time together as husband and wife, having fun and sharing feelings, is not detrimental to the children. Ultimately they will develop confidence in their new family as they witness a growing trust and love between their father and stepmother. Many stepmothers told me that they have a date alone with their husband at least once a month, and some dated once a week. They spent time walking, skiing, boating, going out to dinner, biking, and all kinds of other activities that provided time alone together as a couple. This time alone deepened their love for each other and strengthened their sense of togetherness.

When Don and I first married, we promised each other that we would have a date alone once a week. It was our private time to get to know each other as people, not as parents. We tried not to use that time to talk about the children, but to focus our attention on each other as any newlywed couple would. Sometimes our date was a breakfast date, sometimes dinner. Our weekly date became so important that we have continued the practice to this very day. I remember a few financially lean times when our date was a walk together or a trip to Taco Bell for a soft drink. What we did, where we went, or what we ate were never as important to us as was having time to be alone together and talk.

### Minimal Contact

The second characteristic of happily remarried couples is that they experience minimal conflict in their relationship. How can Mom No. 2 reduce conflict in her marriage? The surest way is to marry someone with similar values.

The Bible says, "Do not be yoked together with unbelievers. For what do righteousness and wickedness have in common?" (2 Cor 6:14). There will be more conflict if one spouse is committed to loving and obeying God, and the other is not. If Mom No. 2 is a Christian who married a non-Christian, she can expect frequent disagreements. She has set herself up for tough times by marrying someone who does not share her faith in God. The Bible tells her not to abandon her marriage but to handle conflict with her husband by living a pure and holy life, loving him gently that she might win him over to faith in Christ (1 Pt 3:1-4). When Mom No. 2 and her husband share the same love for Christ, and have one spirit and one purpose (Phil 2:1,2), they will discover the secret of marital harmony.

Conflict is born out of the different values that Mom No. 2 and her husband have developed out of their separate family backgrounds, training, and life experiences. When differences of opinion surface, it would help them to talk together about why they see the issue differently. What were they taught as children? What experiences have they had with this issue before? As a Christian couple, they would need to ask, "What does the Bible say about this matter?" Such discussions help us to understand our own belief systems and to reevaluate them together in light of God's Word.

Mom No. 2 and her husband would experience minimal conflict and maximum joy if they would follow the Bible's advice on how Christians are to get along with one another. Think about what the following "one anothers" would mean to a stepmother's marriage if she and her husband put them into practice:

- love one another (Jn 13:34)
- honor one another above yourselves (Rom 12:10)
- stop passing judgment on one another (Rom 14:13)

- pursue the building up of one another (Rom 14:19)
- accept one another (Rom 15:7)
- serve one another in love (Gal 5:13)
- carry each other's burdens (Gal 6:2)
- be patient, bearing with one another (Eph 4:2)
- be kind and compassionate to one another (Eph 4:32)
- forgive each other (Eph 4:32)
- comfort one another (1 Thes 4:18)
- encourage one another (1 Thes 4:18)
- confess your sins to one another (Jas 5:16)
- pray for one another (Jas 5:16)

Imagine the difference in a marriage where these commands were fulfilled! Marital conflict would cease; families would be whole and happy! When Mom No. 2 gives the needs of her husband priority, looking out for his interests (Phil 2:3,4) and when he does the same for her, then they'll be on the right track to a happy marriage!

### Shared Decision-Making

Don told me before we ever married that he understood his role as my husband as helping me to become all that God wanted me to be. This perspective was very new to me! I had been raised to understand the wife's role as that of supporting her husband ("the woman behind the man"), but it never occurred to me that a husband would assume an equally supportive role with his wife.

As we have studied the Scriptures, Don and I have seen how God has always intended husbands and wives to work together. He created both men and women in his image (Gn 1:27) and ordained that they rule over the earth together (Gn 1:28). Though sin disrupted and distorted this relationship (Gn 3:16), in Christ the husband/wife relationship is redeemed. In Christ, men and women are freed from sin's distortions and able to enjoy equality (Gal 3:27). They become joint-heirs in Christ, submitting to each other out of reverence for Christ (1 Pt 3:7, Eph 5:21). Don and I have experienced a joy that comes from growing *together* as Christians, supporting and encouraging each other in tough times, and helping each other to be more effective in our family and professional roles.

Happily remarried couples work together toward common goals as they make decisions together, respecting each other's opinions and feelings. They parent together, they care for their home together, and they serve others together.

Anne describes her relationship with her husband this way: "God brought us together and he guides us through the good and the bad together. We listen to each other, we spend time with each other, and we love each other." Though they've been married four years now, Anne says, "We're still on our honeymoon because we don't take each other for granted."

## HAVING FUN TOGETHER

I planned every detail very carefully. I made provision for someone to care for the kids and the dog, I reserved a secluded mountain cabin, I bought a few groceries, I filled the gas tank, I packed the suitcases, and I waited. He never knew what hit him!

When Don walked into the house that Friday night, he never suspected a thing. Little did he know that he was about to be kidnapped! I marched my trusting husband out to my car, opened the passenger side and told him to get in. I quickly took the wheel and, with a perplexed husband by my side, drove away into the night! We arrived an hour and a half later at a mountain cabin where Don built a beautiful fire in the fireplace while I fixed a crab legs dinner for two. Our weekend was quiet, romantic, and wonderful! And when we returned home, Don loved telling our friends about his experience as a "kept" man!

A good dose of spontaneity and adventure, along with lots of laughter, make a fine recipe for a happy marriage. Mom No. 2 should plan times for just plain fun with her whole family and with her husband alone. Laughter refreshes the soul and times of lighthearted play bring needed perspective and strength when the going gets tough. "A cheerful heart is good medicine" (Prv 17:22) for all of life, and especially for a marriage! A good marriage is a marvelous gift from God—celebrate His gift!

# SEVEN

# Your Place or Mine?

*As you think about where to live, practicality is only one consideration; emotional cost is another, and it is equally important. Living in either her place or his can create problems. As the newcomers move in, some stepfamily members feel intruded upon; the rest feel like intruders. Emotional ghosts—uneasy reminders of the previous spouse—are not easily evicted. The situation can become a catch-22: changing things upsets the bereaved children, leaving things alone, the new spouse.*

**Strengthening Your Stepfamily**
**Elizabeth Einstein and Linda Albert**

"I SAW TOO MANY GHOSTS in that house," she said, "and I wanted to be somewhere else. I just wanted it to be our house!"

"Wait a minute," I replied, "I thought when you got married you moved into his *new* house. His first wife never even lived there, did she?"

"No," was her answer, "she didn't. Still, I felt the need to start over completely fresh in our own house."

After that conversation, I realized again how deeply affected many women are by their surroundings—how much a woman's home is connected to her sense of identity and well-being. This stepmother was threatened by reminders of the first wife in a house where the first wife had never even lived! Where stepfamilies decide to live is a major issue, especially for the stepmother.

Some couples make the decision on housing with practical concerns taking priority. Perhaps only one of them owns a house, so they live there. If they both own homes, they may choose to live in the larger house—the one with the most bedrooms. They also may choose to keep the one that is largely paid for. Sometimes they choose to live in a house because of its location in a certain school district. Practical considerations are important, but they are only part of the picture.

When Fran married Rob, she was an established career single. She had worked hard and long to own her own home and furnish it according to her own taste. Rob, whose wife had died of cancer, had lived in his home for many years and still had two grown children with him. Both homes were well-located and well-furnished. Either one would have met the practical needs of this new stepfamily. Yet, to both Fran and Rob, both homes represented their past. They wanted a new beginning. They sold both of them, bought a new home, and mingled and redistributed their furnishings throughout. It was a lot of work, a lot of hassle. But it was emotionally necessary for them to feel they were moving forward with their lives. Sometimes emotional needs legitimately outweigh the practical ones.

Don and I didn't discuss where we would live after the wedding, because our choice was obvious. He owned a house, a fair amount of furniture, and I owned almost nothing. I gathered up my few things and moved in. I freely admit, there were times when I felt like an intruder. Clearly, another woman had settled that nest. Her presence was felt in every room.

This type of experience can make stepmothers feel like outsiders, peripheral to the family. For this reason, most stepfamily counselors recommend moving to a new house. The new house says, "This is a new family. We're all beginning this new life together. We are all on equal footing. What do we want our family to be?"

But, for some families, moving would be difficult, either financially or logistically. That was the case for us, so I moved into Don's house. I remember feeling like I was in someone else's home. Not wanting to hurt my family's feelings, I kept my thoughts about the house to myself. But deep inside, I longed to feel that I was in my own home, one that belonged to me too.

If you must move into an existing home, where your husband and his children live, your concern should be that everyone's space is respected. Space represents belonging. The house belongs to the whole family, but everyone has his or her own individual space. The children's bedrooms represent their space, physical and psychological. A wise stepmother does not begin by invading the children's already established territory. If Mom No. 2 brings her own children to a second marriage, space conflicts can be monumental. If possible, she should keep children in their own rooms and avoid doubling up. The children's need for privacy may never be greater than in the first few years of stepfamily life. Because preserving bedroom space is centrally important to the development of positive feelings towards Mom No. 2, stepbrothers and stepsisters, and half brothers and half sisters, where to live *must* be discussed prior to marriage. If necessary, choose less square footage and more bedrooms over more square footage with fewer bedrooms. Involve all the children in this choice.

Mom No. 2 should feel free to redecorate the existing home according to her own taste, but she should not move too quickly. Happily, despite my youth and inexperience, I made changes in the house slowly. I'm thankful that I demonstrated a modicum of wisdom as I began the careful process of making Don's home our home. I started with the master bedroom. The bedroom represented the new intimacy that Don and I would share as husband and wife. It was extremely important to me that the bedroom be new. So, Don and I gave each other a very wise wedding gift. We went shopping for new bedroom furniture before we married. The new bed and two dressers were delivered while we were away on our honeymoon. When we came home, we gave the bedroom walls a fresh coat of paint, bought new drapes and a matching bedspread, and unpacked our belongings into brand-new furniture. I felt like a new bride, and Don felt like a new groom. We enjoyed our first project together and we did not disrupt the children's lives by remodeling our bedroom. I think the new bedroom was a symbol of the newness of our marriage. I did not feel like a second wife. I felt like a new bride.

My second project, several months later, was to overhaul the kitchen. A wife and mother spends a great deal of time in the kitchen. I know that once I had settled the kitchen, I would feel even more at home, even more a part of the family. Changes in the kitchen were not threatening to the children either. They expected that I would rearrange it to suit my needs and tastes. I began by emptying out all the cupboards and scrubbing everything in sight. Next, I sorted through the kitchen contents, discarding duplicate or needless items. Then I had fun deciding where to store everything—silverware, dishes, pots and pans, towels, and food. I settled the kitchen in a way that I understood and that made meal preparation easier for me.

Our budget was very limited in our first years of marriage, so creativity and economy were critical to sprucing up the kitchen. But, as my mother often said, "It's amazing what you can do with a can of paint and a little fabric!" She was right! I bought some pale yellow paint and repainted the kitchen. It was so little that when I stepped back to admire my work on one wall, I backed into the wall behind me! I then owned a fashionable pair of jeans with a yellow seat!

Once the walls were painted, I bought a few yards of cotton percale fabric and made some new kitchen curtains. Though my expenses were modest, I loved the final product. The little kitchen looked cheerful and inviting. Don and the children liked the new look too.

I think that new stepmothers should begin redecorating projects in their "emotional centers" in the house. For me, they were the master bedroom and the kitchen. With time, moving slowly, we painted the bathroom, the living room, and some bedrooms. We included the children in decisions that affected common living areas or their own bedrooms. This reinforced our understanding that the house belonged to all of us. Working on it together gave us a sense of shared pride.

A complicating factor related to this "new space/old space," "your place/my place" problem is that most stepmothers do not have their stepchildren living with them full-time. Nine times as many women stepmother part-time as stepmother full-time. According to author Charles Cerling: "Visiting stepchildren create special challenges. They bring far more stress into your life than full-time stepchildren. As a full-time stepmother, over time, you work out your differences with your spouse's children. While you might not be close, you can work out a functional relationship. Because you spend so little time with your visiting stepchildren, your relationship may never reach a tension-free stage."[1]

Part-time stepmothering has unique challenges. If the husband's divorce was particularly bitter, visitation schedules and circumstances can become nasty arenas for competition between the divorced parents. This makes visitation with their father and stepmother even more stressful for the children. Making the transition between two homes can be very tough on them. They must adjust to two different homes with different rules, different routines, different expectations, and different personalities.

A recent television special focused on the stresses of stepfamily life. For the children, bouncing back and forth between homes was the hardest part of their parent's divorce. The children wanted to spend time with both of their natural parents, but life was unsettled when they lived in two places.

For some children, however, living in two homes can work well. Steve and Tim, ages twelve and nine, told me they liked having two homes: "You can meet more friends and you get to spend more time with your parents. They show you more attention. We do fun things at both houses!"

One of the ways to ease the stress your visiting stepchildren feel is to provide them space of their own in your home. This may be difficult to do if you are living in a small home or apartment, but remember that having his or her own space says to the child, "You belong here." When stepmothers treat children like guests in their father's home, the children feel like the intruders. Sleeping on a sofa, living out of a suitcase, having nowhere to keep things, makes children feel as though they do not belong—as though there is no room for them in the father's new life. They may feel unwanted and unloved.

Stepmothers Elizabeth Einstein and Linda Albert offer practical suggestions to help visiting children feel part of the stepfamily:

> ... parents can provide a permanent space for each child— a room, corner, cupboard, or drawer—depending on the space available. They can display children's artwork year-round, whether the children are there or not. They can include the children in family plans, made by letter or telephone if a child can't be present to be consulted. Belonging, learning, contributing: this trio fosters psychological and emotional well-being.[2]

Stepmothers should also give the children a little breathing space. Allow them time to adjust when they come for the weekend, or the week, or the summer. Whatever the schedule, children need some time to adjust to the new place before they're ready to relate to the family. Some children may be feeling guilty for leaving their mother to go and be with their father and his new wife. Give them time to sort through their feelings. When they leave your home, don't add to these guilt feelings. Instead, let them know how much you enjoyed their time with you, how much you are eagerly awaiting the next time, and then encourage them to enjoy the time they will spend at their mother's until you see them again. Try to relieve the children of extra pressure and guilt as they move between the two homes.

Most of all, reassure the children. Permanence is the key issue. You let them know that they are a permanent part of your life by providing them a place of their own in your home, but don't forget to verbally communicate your care for them as well. Let them know that you are committed to your relationship with them; that as far as you are concerned this relationship is forever, allowing them to read permanence in both the physical security of their own space in your home and in your verbal assurance that you will be there for them as long as they need you.

We found out how important having a new home was in our own marriage when one year and eight months after we were married, Don assumed a new teaching position in Colorado. When we left New York, we left the past. We were beginning a new adventure as a family. Our first house in Colorado was very modest and sparsely furnished, but it was the first house that was new to all of us and I loved it! I learned how liberating a geographic move can be! God gave us the gift of a fresh start. We were now Don, Beth, and kids. While it was obvious that I was not Mom No. 1 to the children, new friends were content with a brief explanation and they easily accepted my role as Mom No. 2. Sharing the details of our family's history was unnecessary. We began a new chapter in our lives together. *Our house* symbolized a new feeling of belonging, a new identity as family. We had a place of our own!

# EIGHT

# Before I Came and Now That I'm Here

*Being in the parental position but never being the real parent seems to be harder on women than it is on men. The stepmother is left feeling as though her nose is pressed against the window while the real party goes on inside without her.*

**The Good Stepmother: A Practical Guide**
**Karen Savage and Patricia Adams**

I REMEMBER SITTING at the dinner table, listening to Don and the children talk about events that occurred before I married into the family. Sometimes they'd talk about family gatherings in Oregon, or life together in California, or family vacations. Sometimes they'd talk about Grandma Brown— her warmth, her intelligence, her wit, and her strong will. Kay and David happily recalled how she always had a good supply of candy on hand for her grandchildren. Grandma Brown died before I even met Don. She sounded wonderful. I wished I could have known her.

This early table talk made me feel both happy and sad. I was happy to learn more about the family history, but I was also saddened by it. These memories didn't include me and I often felt left out, like an outsider looking in. There is no avoiding the fact that when a woman becomes a stepmother, she lives with the results of an early family history that shaped her husband and his children before she became their wife and stepmother. Knowing this history gives Mom No. 2 valuable insight into her family. Yet, it also reminds her she is not Mom No. 1.

If a family's early years were painful, the stepmother must live with the subsequent problems. When Diane married Jack, he was the divorced father of two children. After spending thousands of dollars and enduring a messy court battle, Jack obtained limited visitation rights. Diane knew that marrying Jack meant occasional stepmothering for a week or two every summer. Then life changed suddenly and drastically for Diane and Jack.

Two and a half years after the wedding, when Diane was seven and a half months pregnant with her first child, Jack's ex-wife died. Jack left immediately to comfort his children and to bring them home to live with him. When the maternal grandparents objected to Jack's desire for custody, Jack spent several thousand dollars more on his legal battle to raise his own children. Jack won custody only after a great deal of stress and expense.

Diane's world turned upside down. With just one week's notice, she became full-time stepmother to a seven-year-old daughter and a five-year-old son. The nursery, decorated for her new baby, was quickly converted to a bedroom for Jack's two children.

To make things worse, these children had not received much attention in their early years. They were unhappy and hostile. They fought fiercely with each other. The stepdaughter threw tantrums; the stepson tried to poison the dog. Diane's dream of her happy little family, husband, wife, and new baby, was shattered.

At first Diane was bitter and resentful. She had to care for two more children. She was about to deliver her first baby. They were crowded for space in their small home. She and

Jack had enormous debt because of the custody battles, forcing Jack to take a second job to meet their expenses. From dawn until dark, Diane stayed at home with two, young, difficult children to handle by herself.

She faced a tough decision. She could either accept her new role as stepmother or resent it. She could leave, but she loved Jack very much and was soon to have his baby. Life was painful. With time, Diane decided that if her marriage was going to work, she must accept the reality of his two children as part of the family and make the best of things.

Diane inherited stepchildren with a tough background. Their early years with their first mother were times of conflict and instability. They felt rejected by their mother when she died. The children displaced their anger toward their mother onto Diane. But Diane remained committed to them. She sought professional help to unravel and understand the children's early history. She determined to give them a happier and more secure future if they would only let her.

Diane began by establishing clear boundaries, explaining what behavior was okay and not okay in the family. Then she engaged in the hard work of consistently enforcing the rules. She allowed the children their anger, but they could not express it by hurting each other. She ignored her stepdaughter's tantrums as long as she was not hurting herself or others. After a while, the tantrums stopped. Diane gave her stepchildren responsibilities appropriate to their ages. She also worked to create happy memories for them, planning many moments of family play together. Although it has been hard work, she has refused to give up on her stepchildren. As a result she has not only seen their hostility decline, she has actually come to love them!

Diane feels that she has invested so much in these children that it is sometimes hard to accept her role as Mom No. 2. When the children want to talk about Mom No. 1, she becomes a good listener. She knows that they need to talk about their first mother in order to understand themselves, but she admits, "It's hard. I've been through so much with them. I wish they were just mine." Every day, she deals with the reality of Mom No. 1 and the unhappy life that her children lived in their formative years.

From the very beginning, stepmothers know that family history is a strong force in their home. The nagging question is: "How am I measuring up against that history?" As Charles Cerling describes it: "As a stepparent, you never simply react. Every time you act, others sit in judgment on what you do. Your stepchildren compare it with life in the home they grew up in. Your spouse compares it with what he did before you came on the scene."[1] When a stepmother hears objections from the children that start with, "But my mother... ," her heart sinks. She hasn't measured up.

How does a stepmother come to terms with her family's past? How can she make peace with her role as Mom No. 2, a Mom that was not there from the family's beginning?

1) *Understand that memories are important.* Memories are important to children who have experienced loss through death or divorce in their families. In children's eyes, the past may appear better than the present. Both of their parents were still together: they lived in a familiar home and neighborhood, and felt like part of a "normal family." Stepmother Cynthia Lewis-Steere reminds us that "children *need* yesterdays to hold onto, so don't be alarmed if they sometimes seem to be living in the past. Chances are, the kids don't *intentionally* set out to irritate you when they pull out the old family photo album and pore over it for hours."[2] As stepmothers, we cannot afford to take personally all the behaviors of our stepchildren. When they talk about their past, we cannot assume they are rejecting their present, rejecting us. Reviewing their history is one way for children to come to terms with both their past and present.

As my stepchildren have entered their adult years, they have talked more about their first mother than they did when they were younger. Understanding their relationship with her is important to them in understanding themselves. Acknowledging her role in their lives in no way diminishes my role. While I know this to be true, I confess that discussing her occasionally makes me wish that I had been their Mom No. 1 all along. Sometimes our hearts need time to catch up with our heads.

Noncustodial stepmothers walk a fine line when it comes to learning about their stepchildren's past. Joyce's two stepchildren visit every other weekend. "It's hard to pick up these kids in 'midstream'," she confided. "I wanted to know more about them, about their past, but I felt like I 'violated' them by digging for information." Joyce had asked the children not to tell their mother everything that happened while they stayed with Joyce, but that meant she had to respect their mother's privacy as well, not invading it with too many questions. Joyce tried to set more objective boundaries between the two homes. Her stepchildren could share from their past as they wanted. The children chose what past events they wanted to talk about and Joyce learned not to probe.

2) *Be aware of the stronger influence of family history on older stepchildren.* Older children obviously have a more developed sense of family history and tradition than do younger ones. They have a keen sense of the "right" way and the "wrong" way of doing things, based on the way things were done in the family before there was a stepmother. They know what time dinner should be served, what foods are best liked, how Sunday afternoons should be spent, what kids should be expected to do around the house, whether or not you eat your Thanksgiving dinner in the middle of the day or in the evening, or whether or not you open presents on Christmas Eve or Christmas morning. Older children may appear less flexible than younger ones, simply because they have experienced certain traditions for more years. Respect how difficult change can be for them.

Many children are expected to handle major changes on a

regular basis. When Joan married Craig, his oldest son came to live with them on a regular basis. But Craig's other two children split their time between their mother's and their father's homes. When they are with their mother, they have few rules or responsibilities. But when they live with Craig and Joan, they must abide by clearly defined family rules. They need to share bedrooms and keep them clean, share computer games, feed the dogs, keep a curfew, and attend church. At first, the children protested loudly and rebelled against these restrictions, but with time they began to see that these responsibilities were their assurance of truly belonging to the family. These expectations, so difficult to live with initially, are becoming routine.

3) *Make changes slowly.* As you create new traditions as a stepfamily, make these changes slowly. I found that new traditions that did not compete with old ones were best. Instead of threatening family history, I added to it.

Don tells me that I added more celebrations to the family. This does not surprise me, as I have a tendency to celebrate life in general. Before I married Don, he and David used to watch Sunday afternoon football games together, while the females in the house disappeared to do other things. After we were married, I joined them in watching the games although I knew amazingly little about football. David bought me a book that explained the rules of the game, and I became more and more enthusiastic about the sport. Sunday afternoon football games became a weekly celebration! We popped some corn and sat around yelling at the game on television and cheering the players on to victory. Today, I've become what's known in Denver as a "Bronco-maniac."

Tree-trimming at Christmastime also became a celebration. Don remembers that before I came into the family, he used to put up the tree alone. It was simply a chore to be done. After we were married, I instituted a tree-trimming party. I'm embarrassed to admit that our first party got off to a shaky start when I had my first major disagreement with my new husband. Don was hanging the tree lights so that they were showing on the tops of the branches, and I thought they should be more hidden among the branches. It was a big deal to me then for some reason, which shows how strong emotions can be over the tiniest clash of traditions. Thankfully, we worked out the "Great Christmas Tree Light Controversy" and continued on with our party. We played Christmas carols, strung cranberries and popcorn garlands, hung ornaments and tinsel, and then sipped hot chocolate while enjoying the beauty of the tree and Christmas. Tree-trimming became a celebrated tradition in my new family. I remember these family times so fondly that I now rush to put up our tree soon after Thanksgiving so that I can enjoy both the tree and the pleasant memories it evokes.

When I became Mom No. 2, I made a big splash of birthdays—something that none of the children seemed to mind! I'd have balloons, crepe paper streamers, a home-made personalized cake, and lots of presents! I really fussed over each child as a way of celebrating their presence in our family.

On Valentine's Day, later in my married life, I gave a Valentine to each child, reminding them of my love for them. I'd place a small gift at their plate at the dinner table. Valentine's Day became more than a celebration as a couple; it became a reminder of the love we shared as a family.

None of these changes threatened earlier family traditions; they simply added to them.

4) *Value and learn from each other's histories.* We stepmothers should remember that we bring our own histories and traditions into the family as well. Everyone in the family is being exposed to new experiences, new ideas, new values. By listening to one another, and accepting each other's different histories, all of our lives can be enriched. Stepmothers Elizabeth Einstein and Linda Albert write: "As they learn alternative ways of thinking and behaving, people in stepfamilies gain a broader view of life and teach each other helpful living skills. Acceptance helps merge two families into one."[3]

Nick was only eleven when his mother told him he was "uncontrollable" and kicked him out. From now on, he would have to live with his father and his father's new wife, Evelyn. This little boy's hostility and insecurity caused problems from the first. The road to a functional relationship has been rough and rocky, but there are an increasing number of good days to offset the bad ones. Interestingly, Evelyn's family history was important in helping Nick both to accept himself and to warm to his new stepmother.

Evelyn's family is full of tradition. Her parents are Iowa farmers who have always had a close relationship with their children and extended family. Christmas, for example, is a huge family reunion. Oyster stew and chili are served on Christmas Eve. Christmas morning begins early with farm chores, followed by the opening of gifts and a huge farm breakfast. Evelyn's parents have welcomed Nick as part of the family and he loves spending time with them on the farm, where a rich tradition of a warm family life is helping Nick deal with his earlier lack of love, disappointment, and anger.

5) *Give yourself time to develop a new family history.* The best antidote for feeling left out of each other's lives because of separate histories, is to create a shared history. This takes time. As I look back over the twenty-three years of my married life, I can now recall many happy memories that I've shared with the children. I can also remember the hard times—times of financial stress, times when children were sick, the night our house caught on fire. The good times and the bad have become our new family history. I'm a part of it all. I no longer feel like I'm on the outside looking in. This new family life is the result of learning to know and accept each other, learning to respect each other's differences, changing our expectations of each other, and negotiating new ways to live our lives.

The separate histories that existed before marriage do not miraculously blend together into one history when you are pronounced "husband and wife." In fact, families in second marriages rarely blend in any fashion; those separate histories will always exist for everyone. But a new history can create close relationships among the members of a stepfamily.

The children will always remember events in their lives that occurred before they knew me, but I know they will also remember a wealth of memories fashioned by our life together.

# NINE

# Loving Enough to Discipline

*Discipline doesn't break a child's spirit half as often as the lack of it breaks a parent's heart.*

14,000 Quips and Quotes
**E.C. McKenzie**

THE JOY OF DISCIPLINE is not in its practice but in its results! Only a sadistic parent would enjoy correcting a child's misbehavior, but every conscientious parent delights in the disciplined child whose behavior reflects spiritual commitment, integrity, and care for others.

## FEARING DISCIPLINE

Stepmothers often fear the practice of discipline. When a woman marries a man with children, she knows that the success of her marriage will be measured, in part, by her ability to be a good parent to his children. Christian mothers want to model their parenting after the Heavenly Father who disciplines his children because he loves them (Heb 12:6).

A mother who loves her children disciplines them. But if a *step*mother disciplines her children, will she be perceived as loving, or as the cruel, mean "wicked stepmother?" *"What* *will everybody think* if I discipline the children? And, most of all, what will the children think about me?" the stepmother wonders. This fear of rejection can keep her from participating assertively in discipline.

Stepmothers want their husband's children to respect, accept, and even love them. When I first became Mom to ten-year-old Kay, I sincerely loved her. However, my love for her was a new love, and I felt insecure. Kay was very accepting of me when I was her new adult friend across the street, and then her Dad's date, and then his fiancée. Would she love me as her new mother? Oh, I hoped so!

Because I wanted Kay to love me, I was fearful when the time came for me to correct her for the first time. She was just a little girl, and sometimes she fussed when she wanted something, as many little girls do. I asked her to use a pleasant tone of voice when she wanted something, promising always to answer her if she did, but not to answer if she used a fussy voice. Then I followed through. "Ask me again in your pleasant voice," I'd say calmly. She was frustrated but would repeat her request for me in her best "grown up" voice. Inside, I hoped beyond hope that she wouldn't hate me for my insistence.

Within two short weeks, that little girl's fussy voice completely disappeared, and a consistently sweet voice took its place forever. This was a tiny matter, but my fear of Kay's rejection was enormous! While this incident was threatening to me, it made little impression on Kay. Now, as my grown daughter, she tells me that she doesn't even remember this happening! She confides, "I honestly don't remember being disciplined much by you. I know that I was, but it was obviously no big deal since nothing really stands out." She remembers that I loved her—that's what she remembers!

This story illustrates how easy it is for a stepmother to develop an irrational fear of a disciplinary role. Fortunately, Kay had been loved and disciplined in her early years, and she knew that love and discipline were intertwined. She accepted my discipline as a natural part of my role as her mother. In doing so, she accepted my love for her.

Fathers can fear discipline as well, particularly those fathers in stepfamilies born of divorce. Joyce's husband, Matt, was overcome with guilt about the pain that he had caused his children when he divorced their mother. From now on he wanted the children's life to be wonderful. Matt simply could not discipline his children; it made him feel terrible to do so! Early in their marriage, Joyce was left to discipline her stepchildren on her own. She describes her stepchildren as "good kids" who needed little discipline. But at those moments when they acted out some of their anger and frustration, she knew they needed some firm correction. Joyce knew that loving them meant disciplining them, but she needed her husband's support. Wisely, this couple got professional counseling. When Matt came to terms with his divorce and found personal healing, he was again able to participate in disciplining his children.

Stan is another father who feared disciplining his child. Stan's young son, Nick, came to live with him soon after his marriage to Evelyn. Nick was very angry and resented his new stepmother. He worked to drive a wedge between his father and Evelyn by misbehaving during the day and then denying anything had happened when his father got home from work in the evening. Evelyn was hurt by Nick's disrespect for her and worried that the tension Nick created would threaten the stability of her new marriage.

Nick's disrespect for others and lack of self-discipline, in Evelyn's words, "drove her crazy." Life with Nick was tough. As a Christian, Evelyn understood that loving Nick meant disciplining him. He needed discipline for his own well-being, now and in the future. Evelyn explained her motives: "My goal was not to make him miserable. I just wanted Nick to be a decent kid who could make good decisions."

But Stan didn't want to add any more pain to Nick's life.

He was struggling with his own guilt over divorcing his son's mother. As a Christian he felt that he had failed Nick. Not wanting to hurt him any more, Stan preferred leniency and felt that Evelyn was expecting too much of this young boy.

Stan and Evelyn sought the advice of a Christian counselor. Evelyn came to understand that Nick's hostility wasn't really about her, but about his own feelings of rejection. Stan faced his feelings of guilt, and while Stan is still more lenient than Evelyn, he is beginning to handle the discipline more and is supportive of Evelyn's parental role. Together, they are asking God to help them be better parents. Stan and Evelyn learned how important it is that divorced fathers overcome their feelings of failure after a broken first marriage. Only after Stan had experienced his Heavenly Father's loving discipline and forgiveness, could he assume a healthy parental role in discipline.

## DISCIPLINE'S PURPOSE

Stepmothers will fear the children's rejection less as they become convinced of the ultimate purpose of discipline. Discipline is the means by which a child comes to understand, value, and live by Christian truth. When the Apostle Paul wrote to young Timothy, his son in the faith, Paul encouraged Timothy to be "nourished on the words of faith and sound doctrine" (1 Tm 4:6 NAS). Paul explained that such discipline produces godliness (v.7), and godliness not only enriches the present life but also benefits the eternal life to come. Disciplined children can become living examples of God's love in "speech, conduct, love, faith, and purity" (v.12). That's a tall order and one that's difficult to remember in the hard times of discipline. Yet disciplined children are the only ones who are able to experience the fullness of God's joy as they negotiate life's struggles! Disciplined children, anchored in God's truth, are better prepared to cope with life's challenges!

Discipline is a profound expression of love. When Mom No. 2 disciplines her stepchild, she is saying, "Your father and I care about you. We care about your ability to handle life well. We care about your character, about your integrity, about your present well-being, and about your eternal future." Lack of parental discipline says to a child, "You're not worth the effort. You can just grow up on your own. We'll take our chances on how you turn out."

When Evelyn chose to work hard at changing Nick's behavior, she demonstrated her care for him. She faced his anger head on because she knew that his life would be unhappy forever until he learned obedience. Although her new role as a stepmother was hard and often discouraging, she knew that love meant participating with her husband in shaping Nick's life.

## THE STEPMOTHER'S ROLE IN DISCIPLINE

The stepmother's role in disciplining the stepchildren will depend, in part, on the ages of the children. Young children seem to adjust more easily to the disciplinary role of their stepmother. Diane's stepchildren were only five and seven years old when she entered the family. Their natural mother had died and Diane became their central mother figure. Because of this, she disciplined the children from the very beginning.

Ruth also had two young stepchildren and, like Diane, she exercised discipline from the beginning with her husband's strong support. That doesn't mean it was easy. She remembers the first time she had to paddle the boys. They were playing wildly in the bathtub, sliding around and splashing water everywhere. Ruth told them to settle down before one of them got hurt, but they didn't, and she finally had to spank them.

Ruth had perfectly good reasons for doing what she did: She was concerned for their safety, she was afraid they would fall and get hurt, and she was the responsible adult present. All good reasons, but what she remembers most is how hard it was for her! No one enjoys disciplining children, and it is even harder for a stepmother than for anyone else. Being a "good stepmother" is not easy!

My son, David, speaks from the child's side. At the moment of discipline, the child is not happy either. David tells me, "It was difficult at times to accept discipline from you. Not usually, but sometimes. You wouldn't let me get away with some things that Dad would. Even though I let it get to me sometimes, it never affected my feelings toward you or my desire to have you with me." Children have a way of knowing that discipline is meant for their good, even when they don't like it.

Not surprisingly, adolescents have the toughest time accepting discipline from a stepmother. Older children are in the process of separating from parental control, so trying to add more control is very threatening to them. When dealing with adolescents, leaving the disciplining to the natural parent is probably wisest. Stepmothers should move slowly, allowing time to develop a rapport with teen-age stepchildren.

Many stepmothers make this choice to leave the disciplining of the older children to the father, and are content to develop a friendship, rather than a parental relationship, with adolescents. This was certainly the only choice open to me. I was too close in age to Don's three oldest children. It would have been foolish and unrealistic to think I could be a parent to them; so I chose to be their friend in whatever ways they would let me.

Rick, age eighteen, and Sharon, age seventeen, were comfortable in a friendship relationship with me. I think because Sharon was a young woman, it was easiest to become close to her. We had more interests to share and enjoyed spending time together. Steve, age fifteen, resisted even a friendship with me. He was smack in the middle of his adolescent identity crisis which was only complicated by the addition of a young stepmother in his life. When Don and I married, Rick had already left home and Sharon was a high school senior soon to be headed for college. When Steve needed any discipline, Don took charge completely. It would have been presumptuous and unnatural for me to do so.

Even when a stepmother approximates the age of the absent natural mother, teen-age stepchildren are unlikely to accept her as a disciplinarian. Laura's two teen-age stepsons let her know right away that she "had no right" to discipline them. Because Laura's husband shared his sons' view, Laura left all the disciplining to him.

Joan's husband, Craig, saw things differently. When Joan was first a stepmother, she had no desire to discipline the older children. When the kids misbehaved, she'd wait to tell Craig about what they did so he could handle it. This left Joan feeling like an adult tattletale. Craig encouraged Joan to begin handling some situations herself. Now, in small day-to-day matters, Joan handles the discipline of her teen-agers. She tells them to do their chores, to stop quarreling, to turn down the stereo, or to get home by eleven. Only when major issues arise does she reserve the disciplinary role for their father. Sharing discipline with her husband helped to clarify Joan's role in the family and strengthened her relationship with her teen-age children. Joan plays a greater disciplinary role in her stepfamily than Laura, illustrating that every stepfamily is unique and should feel comfortable working out their own solutions to discipline in the home.

## A UNITED FRONT

Second marriages usually fail because of conflict over the discipline of the children. For a stepfamily to find stability and happiness, the father and the stepmother must *stand to-*

*gether* in their roles as parents. Couples must *agree* on family expectations, how they will be enforced, and who will do the enforcing. As the Juroes explain: "Unless roles are clearly identified, some stepparents are going to feel timid about their stepchild. And, some natural parents may resent any interference by the stepparent. If you're going to share another person's life and children, then *the two of you must present a united front.*" (emphasis mine)[1]

This truth is sadly depicted by Nancy's story. Nancy divorced her first husband, lived five years as a single parent with her two small children, and then married Frank. Frank also had two children—a teen-age daughter who lived with her mother and an eight-year-old son, Devin, who came to live with Frank and Nancy.

When it came to disciplining Devin, Nancy and Frank never worked as a team. In fact, they worked against each other. When Nancy disciplined Devin, Frank took his son's side. Rather than support his wife's role, Frank would challenge Nancy by asking, "What did you do to set him off?"

One day Nancy asked Devin to clean his room. When Devin refused to obey, Nancy insisted. Devin, then a young teenager, called Frank at work and shouted into the telephone: "This place stinks! I'm going to live with my mother! You come home and take me there!" Frank told Devin not to argue with his stepmother and just to watch television until he could get home. Then he asked to talk to Nancy. With Devin listening in on his extension, Frank told Nancy that she and Devin were not to talk to each other until he got home from work. Then he yelled, "If I don't have a son when I get home, it's your fault!"

Nancy feels caught in a second marriage where neither her husband nor her stepson (not surprisingly) respect her. She says that counseling has helped her "learn how to care for myself emotionally," but she is not getting support from her family. Frank refuses counseling. Nancy is not sure if her marriage will last and, for the present, is simply "marking time," hoping that when Devin grows up and leaves their home things will improve between Frank and her. This faint hope is all she has.

Nancy's unhappy story underscores the primacy of a committed, loving, and supportive marriage relationship as the sturdy foundation for all stepfamily relationships. Marriages can get off to a healthier start through premarital counseling. Attitudes toward discipline should be discussed in these early sessions. June and William Noble suggest that couples discuss every facet of discipline they can imagine *before* they marry, asking themselves:

- What is it that you do or don't like about spanking?
- What other forms of discipline are you for or against?
- Do you mind when they talk back?
- How do you react to hurtful and cutting remarks?
- How do you react to manipulation?[2]

Let me suggest that couples begin by discussing more fundamental concerns such as: What matters most in life? How will we teach those values to our children? What role will each of us play in disciplining our children?

Experts agree that the stepmother should share some part in the discipline of the children. If the father does all of the disciplining, excluding the stepmother, she will be viewed as an intruder and will become emotionally alienated from her stepchildren.

On the other extreme, it is equally damaging to give a stepmother a primary disciplinary role. The natural parent may be frustrated by the behaviors of a particularly difficult child and decide simply to relinquish responsibility to the new wife. In such circumstances, the stepchild will quickly resent the new stepmother, and she will likely feel overwhelmed and angry with both her husband and his child.

The best approach seems to be shared responsibility for disciplining. The father needs to talk with his children before he marries again and express his unequivocal support for the stepmother's authority in the home. Clarifying roles early will lessen the threat of the unavoidable trap described by Cynthia Lewis-Steere: "There's a waiting trap for all new blending ventures—the trap of playing old parent against new—the trap of challenging the outsider who has trod on their turf."[3] When parents stand together, everyone is happier. The natural parent may take the lead, but the stepmother must participate to earn the children's respect and to be of maximum help to them.

Too many parents see discipline as an adversarial relationship between them and their children rather than a cooperative one. A stepmother may be tempted to use her disciplinary authority to compete with her stepchildren for attention from her new husband. This posture begs for problems. Nurturing discipline is never adversarial. An emotionally secure stepmother sees discipline as an opportunity to *understand* and *help* her new children. She loves them enough to discipline them!

Anne was confounded by the deceptive behavior of her adolescent stepdaughter, Jessica. Without asking, Jessica would borrow Anne's clothes and jewelry. Anne was a professional model and her clothes were important to her success. Jessica's intrusion into Anne's privacy was very devastating to Anne. Anne talked to Jessica along with her husband. Their words made no difference. When Jessica continued taking Anne's things, Anne and her husband put a lock on their bedroom door. Jessica climbed through the window.

In desperation, all three headed for family counseling. What Anne learned there gave her a surprising and helpful insight. Jessica took Anne's clothes and jewelry because *she wanted to be like Anne*! Understanding that, Anne was able to give Jessica greater attention and support, while becoming more assertive in protecting her right to privacy. Today, only a few short years later, Anne describes her relationship with

Jessica as very close. Working to change Jessica's behavior was a loving endeavor and increased understanding between stepmother and stepdaughter.

Anne's story ended happily for several reasons. She was committed in her role as Jessica's stepmother. She sought help from a Christian counselor when she needed help, and she *worked with her husband as a team* to understand and help Jessica.

Parents must continually talk with each other about the children and work out their differing approaches to discipline. Author Claire Berman writes that " 'Open communication'... means there must be no covert messages by the parent that the nonparent is to remain uninvolved in the actual raising of the children. The issue must be faced: is the real parent prepared to *share* his children?"[4]

## METHODS OF DISCIPLINE

Children learn to live by Christian values in several ways. Discipline is much more than punishment. Children adopt Christian values as parents teach and model such values.

1. *Reward and punishment.* Throughout the Scriptures, great emphasis is placed on outward behavior. Psalm 15, for example, describes the behavior of a righteous person, a person who lives with integrity and who speaks the truth. Colossians 3:17 tells us we should love God, not only in word, but in deed.

Behaviorist B.F. Skinner made a strong contribution to our understanding of the roles of reward and punishment in shaping children's behavior. One of his most helpful suggestions to parents was that they understand that *reward is more effective than punishment!*

As stepmothers, we are often quick to notice when our stepchildren do things that upset us. While it is important to correct behavior that we think is *wrong*, we could serve our stepchildren even more by noticing the many things that they do *right*! If Mom No. 2 was to affirm *even one* positive behavior a day, the child's behavior would improve dramatically!

When we reward a child's good behavior, our praise must be authentic, or it will fall on deaf ears. Children know when praise is undeserved. Flattery will harm a parent/child relationship; honest praise will strengthen it. Proverbs 28:23 reminds us that honest feedback, even rebuke, builds a relationship. Flattery only tears a relationship apart (Prv 26:28).

Praise will have its greatest power when offered to children for specific expressions of Christian character. This means saying things like, "I liked the way you shared that with your sister," or "What a kind thing you did for your friend when you helped to fix his flat tire," or "Thanks for the help you gave me in getting dinner ready." Discipline means honest praise as well as correction.

When you do need to punish, be sure that you are correcting poor *behavior* only, and not punishing children for expressing their feelings. A good stepmother allows the children to express anger and disappointment but she helps them do this in appropriate ways. Stepparents David and Bonnie Juroe give the following advice: "You must allow the children to express their feelings with complete freedom from retaliation, recrimination, or punishment.... If their behavior is destructive, such as throwing or breaking things, confront them, but still work on allowing the expression of feelings. If you are so insecure that you can't handle their feelings, then you may need to go for help."[5]

Anger in stepchildren is a normal emotion that may result from their experience of loss. Expressing anger may be part of their healing process. Let them talk about their feelings freely, but be alert to when a stepchild may need professional help. If your stepchild exhibits extreme hostility or withdrawal, regularly engages in antisocial behavior, or abuses drugs, you need to get help.

Reward and punishment are effective throughout all of life in changing behavior, but they are especially effective when stepmothering young children. Punish inappropriate behavior consistently and lovingly, but work to reward your stepchildren honestly and generously when they do things right.

**2. *Modeling*.** Disciplining our children requires that we model Christian values in our own lives. Children watch adults closely to see if we do those things that we expect of them. We should be able to tell our stepchildren, just as the Apostle Paul told his spiritual children: "Be imitators of me, just as I also am of Christ" (1 Cor 11:1 NAS). If keeping bedrooms clean is important, then we should model tidiness. If talking respectfully is important, then we should treat our stepchildren with respect. If attending church is important, then we should attend church. In disciplining adolescents, modeling is key. When stepmothers establish standards of behavior for adolescent stepchildren, but do not live by those standards themselves, the battle is lost. This modeling is most powerful in a context of nurture. Teens are more likely to listen to and emulate a stepmother who genuinely expresses love and concern.

There is no way that a stepmother can model perfection. This means that we need to model confession and forgiveness. When we become impatient, when we arrive home later than expected causing our family to worry, when we forget to keep a promise, we need to apologize to our stepchildren and ask them to forgive us. Part of modeling appropriate behavior is modeling what to do when we fail. This allows children to fail too without fearing emotional rejection! This is how children come to experience unconditional love! This is how we model God's gracious and forgiving love in our stepmothering!

**3. *Instruction*.** In addition to punishment, reward, and modeling, stepmothers help their stepchildren learn about

Christian values by teaching them God's Word. Children need to hear about God's love for them. They need to know, personally, that God loves them so much that he sent his Son, Jesus, to die on the cross for their sins (Jn 3:16) and that God offers complete forgiveness to each of us who will trust him (1 Jn 1:9). Sometimes the feelings of grief, guilt, and unworthiness felt among children of loss make it doubly important that they know that their loving Heavenly Father will gladly forgive any wrong, no matter how big or how bad. Not incidently, we must model the same standard of love and forgiveness which God offers us all. After children become Christians, they become life-long disciples, continually learning of God's truth and how this truth is worked out in day-to-day living.

Parents need to discuss attitudes, values, and behaviors with their children as a way of life (Dt 6:5-9). God's truth is to be taught as we share meals together, take trips together, play together, and work together. Stepmothers and fathers need to communicate God's commands clearly and why they think obeying God's commands is important. Children need instruction.

The "what to do" is important. So is the "why we do it." A biblical rationale for our family values is critical if our children are ever going to own these values personally. Our goal in disciplining our children is that someday, when we are no longer around, they will be able to make responsible, godly decisions for themselves. This means that children need to be taught why we study God's Word, why we spend time with other Christians, why we should show respect for others, why we need to share our possessions with others, and why we pray.

Christian values should not only be communicated clearly, they should be communicated early. It is kinder to the children to let them know what your expectations are up front as you begin your new life as a stepfamily. They are less likely to disobey from ignorance. More important, they know early that they are cared for and important to the family. When a stepmother disciplines her stepchild, assigns responsibilities to her stepchild, or takes time to teach her stepchild, she is communicating that this child *belongs* to the family and is *needed* by the family!

When discussing expectations with children, involve them in the process as much as possible. Ask your children, "What would God want us to be like as a family?" When children help decide family rules and the division of family responsibilities, they are more likely to value them and abide by them.


## TESTING GROUNDS

Mom No. 2 should be firm from the very start in establishing her role as disciplinarian. But she should be reasonable. While being too lenient undermines a stepmother's authority, being overly strict and overly demanding can breed resentment in the children. There are times when backing off is the better part of wisdom. Kay illustrates this with one of her childhood memories:

I remember during the first year of our new family, two of my girlfriends were angry with their parents. One girl wanted to run away. This was pretty exciting! I had never contemplated doing anything like this before. We would all save our money. We would rent horses. We would run away. (Who cared that we really didn't know how to ride horses; we were adventurous!) We would only run away for three weeks, so that we wouldn't run out of money. It was decided. We would leave within the month.

Now I had a problem. I didn't want to be left out, but I certainly didn't want to hurt my new Mom's feelings. I was pretty sure that she might take this personally. I should tell her. On the other hand, if I didn't tell her, she couldn't tell me that I couldn't go. (And if she told me I couldn't go, then I knew I'd be in trouble if I did go.) Finally, I decided that her feelings were more important. I remember telling her about our plans to go horseback riding for a few weeks; and that although my girlfriends were running away, I really was just going for the fun of it. I didn't want her to get the idea that I didn't like her or that I was mad at her.

I don't know how I would have handled the situation, but Mom handled it just right. She thanked me for telling her and asked me to let her know if we decided to go ahead and leave so she wouldn't worry about me. Naturally, the plans never did materialize, and I was secretly relieved to tell her that a few weeks later.

Expect children to test the limits of the agreed upon rules and responsibilities. That's normal. Respond firmly and lovingly, and the testing period will run its course. Testing the limits is beneficial: "Once the testing period is over, you should have established a set of behavior expectations that will see you through the long pull. By this time the expectations themselves will have been tested for their usefulness, and all of you... should have a good idea of what will be tolerated within the family."[6]

## THE GOOD NEWS

Most of the stories stepmothers tell about disciplining their stepchildren are stories of pain and struggle. Some have happy endings; many do not. But it would be a grave mistake for a new stepmother to enter her marriage anticipating only problems.

Stepchildren are not unlike natural children in that they can create tension in a marriage. In all marriages, marital satisfaction tends to decrease at the birth of the first child, bottom out as the first child reaches adolescence, and increase dramatically at the empty nest. Raising children takes time and energy. Less attention is given to the relationship between the couple and more attention is given to the children.

Stepchildren, like natural children, can also bring great happiness into a couple's relationship. As Cherie Burns reminds us, "Stepchildren don't have to be detrimental to a marriage. If you are flexible enough to accept the unexpected, your stepchildren may have a positive effect on you and your husband. Sometimes they provide a nice bonus by drawing the two of you together, in much the same way the natural children can convert a couple into a family."[7]

Kay and David were young enough when I married their father that they were able to accept me as a mother in a very short time. They made me feel like I was an important part of their lives, and therefore, an important part of the family.

Nine-year-old David had a talk with his father just a few weeks after our wedding. He began by saying how happy he was that his father had married his new Mom. "How is it that you are so happy, David?" Don asked, pushing for elaboration and expecting David to mention something poetic like how much happier his Dad seemed these days. "Well, Dad," David explained, "I really like the way Mom cooks. I was getting pretty tired of your casseroles!" David had a fine way of getting to the point and making us laugh!

In some ways, I suppose, I'm saying that we stepmothers must learn to take one day at a time. Jesus reminded us that each day had enough trouble of its own, and that we shouldn't waste time today worrying about tomorrow (Mt 6:34). Maybe you feel that you haven't come to the place where you can enjoy your stepchildren; there are so many problems! Let me suggest three things to you.

First, be sure that, as much as possible, you and your husband stand together when it comes to discipline. Discuss your parenting goals with your husband, discuss together your roles in discipline, and view these roles as an expression of love for the children, and for your husband as well.

Second, take one day at a time, but make each day count. Try *daily* to gain a better understanding of your stepchildren. Think of something about your stepchildren that you can be thankful for *daily*. Pray for your children *daily* and find things, even if they are little things, to show your love and commitment for your stepchildren *daily*.

My third suggestion is that you simply persevere. The Scriptures tell us not to become "weary in doing good" (Gal 6:9). What a challenge that is! But how important it is for all of us. So much of life in Christ is based on "keeping on keeping on." One of the most important keys to success as Mom No. 2 is to be *persistent* in love!

# TEN

# And Babies Make Nine...

*The new baby in a blend adds another dimension to a family group searching for its own delicate balance. Suddenly there's a new focus, one without labels or history or one-sided loyalties attached.*

*Stepping Lightly*
**Cynthia Lewis-Steere**

ENTERING MY MOTHER'S HOSPITAL ROOM, I found her sitting up in bed, looking cheerful, and diligently knitting a partially completed baby blanket for my expected new baby, and her first grandchild to be. She was recovering from gall bladder surgery. I had planned to visit Mom that afternoon, but after an early morning appointment with my obstetrician, found that I had a personal reason to visit the hospital that day as well. My doctor had ordered x-rays after he thought that perhaps he heard two fetal heartbeats. Before visiting my mother, I first located the out-patient wing and had a few x-rays taken.

Having found Mom in good spirits, I settled into a bedside chair and made myself as comfortable as possible, considering I was seven and a half months pregnant. I handed her the doctor's order for my x-rays and told her he suspected twins. She gasped and queried, "Honey, don't you ever do anything normally?"

That was a great question. I was a long way from ever knowing "normal" family life, a long way from Blue Heaven's "Honey and me... and baby makes three." I was contemplating my honey, Rick, Sharon, Steve, Kay, and David, and me... and babies make nine!

My conversation with Mom was soon interrupted by a surprise visit from my obstetrician, who was on his rounds at the hospital. Dr. Steiner entered the room, grinning from ear to ear. He gazed at me cheerfully and said, "I just finished looking at your x-rays, Beth, and I'm here to tell you that you're not just expecting one baby. You're carrying twins!"

Somehow that day didn't seem real. I was stunned. So was Mom who cast aside the baby blanket announcing, "I'll never have enough time to finish *two* of these!" Dr. Steiner was so pleased, Mom seemed impressed, but the emotion that flooded over me was just plain fear. I had never had a baby before. I had been taking classes for expectant mothers to build my confidence, but now I would be caring for *two* babies! All of this added to the responsibilities I already had for my new stepchildren at home!

The first thing I needed to do was to tell my husband. I cut short my visit with Mom so I could drive to Don's office and give him the news in person. Easier said than done. When I got out to the hospital parking lot, I discovered that both the cars I had parked between had left and different cars had taken their places. These new cars parked too close to mine, too close for a pregnant lady carrying an extra fifty pounds! I squeezed between the cars, inching my way along until I reached the driver's door. After I got there, I found there wasn't enough room for me to open the door and pry myself in. I worked my way back out and tried the passenger side. Unfortunately that was worse; I couldn't even get to the door. I tried both sides again to no avail. I could feel the tears of frustration welling up in my eyes when the parking lot attendant came running over, laughing so hard that tears ran down his cheeks.

"Lady, I've been watching you from my booth. How would you like me to back your car out for you?"

"Yes, thank you, that would be very nice," I said, trying feebly to muster what little dignity I could as a twenty-two-year-old who was too large to climb inside her car.

The attendant backed my car out of its place. Feeling humiliated but grateful that someone had rescued me, I squeezed behind the wheel. I drove the half hour to Don's office, working to bring my emotions under control. Twins! What an overwhelming thought! What would Don think?

I found my husband in his office, sitting behind his desk. I rushed in, blurting out the news that we were expecting twins! Don laughed his big laugh and hugged me hard! He had always wanted twins, he said, and couldn't be happier! With that, I burst into tears! It was all so overwhelming!

One month later, Amy and April were born, bringing indescribable joy into my life! Two tiny baby girls became part of our family and were to enrich us all in ways we could not imagine! It didn't take long for me to overcome my earlier fears and to firmly believe that having twins was the most wonderful experience any woman could have!

## DECIDING TO ADD A NEW BABY TO THE STEPFAMILY

While we were still dating, Don and I had talked about having children of our own. This is a very important issue to discuss *before* marriage. When the husband is significantly older than his new wife, as was our case, there can be very different feelings about having another child. Some men might be relieved to be through with diapers, late night feedings, and the many demands of small children. Starting all over would be discouraging to them. In our case, Don knew how much I wanted to have a baby, and though the family was already large, he agreed to having more children. Before we ever married, we decided that we wanted to add two children of our own to the family. We didn't know that we'd add two all at once, but that's how it worked out!

Deciding whether or not to have more children can be tough, and the advice is mixed. According to Dr. Fitzhugh Dodson: "In some stepfamilies, the new baby becomes a psychological link between the two families. But in others it can be a negative factor.... Don't decide whether or not to have a child by its possible effect on the stepchildren. Decide it the way you would if you were a husband and wife with no stepchildren to consider. That is, if having a child is important to you and your marriage, then have it. If not, don't."[1]

On the other hand, marriage and family counselor Thelma Kaplan feels differently and suggests that "You should not have the new child while you're still working out your own relationship and those with the present children."[2] There is some truth in both opinions. The couple needs to begin by considering if having a baby is important to them, but they should also evaluate how their decision will affect the other children in the home.

Having a baby is, at first, an individual decision. The husband must ask himself, "Do I want to be a father again?" The wife must ask herself, "Do I want to be a mother?" For some women, this means having a baby for the first time. In the case where each party brings children into the marriage, the wife is asking, "Do I want more children?" When Mom No. 2 enters the marriage without bringing children of her own, there is more likely to be a new baby than when both husband and wife bring children from previous marriages.

Each partner must face his or her own feelings honestly. Then having a baby needs to be discussed as a couple. Is this what we both want, and if so, when would be the best time to have a new baby? In establishing the timing, relationships with the present children should be considered. Everyone needs some time to adjust to the stepfamily dynamics before adjustment to a new baby is added.

Stepfamilies frequently do decide to add a new baby to the picture. According to Frank Furstenberg on the faculty of the University of Pennsylvania, "approximately one-third of all children entering stepfamilies will acquire a half sibling within four years, and close to two-thirds will eventually have either a step- or half sibling."[3] The good news is that the decision to have a baby usually, though not always, turns out to be beneficial to the stepfamily. Stepmother and author Karen Savage reports that, "statistically, stepfamilies that have new children adjust better than stepfamilies who don't."[4]

## AFTER THE BABY ARRIVES

New babies typically bring a fresh unity to the stepfamily, but parents should not make it the *duty* of their mutual children to create unity. When there is family disunity, the responsibility of peacemaking belongs to the parents, not to their mutual child.

A new baby creates family unity symbolically because everyone in the family has a blood tie to the child. The baby is a part of everyone. The new stepmother who felt like an intruder may suddenly feel legitimized. Her new baby now links her to the stepchildren in tangible ways. An enduring, indissoluble bond has been formed between mother and new baby, stepchildren and new baby, and therefore between stepmother and stepchildren. This new legitimacy experienced by stepmothers often boosts their self-confidence. Caring for the needs of the new baby provides a well-defined role for the stepmother and shifts her focus from the more fragile steprelationships.

Mothering the mutual child also helps the stepmother reassess her relationship with her stepchildren. She now has a standard to evaluate whether family occurrences are simply part of raising children, or whether the step dynamic is playing any part at all. Too often, the step dynamic is blamed for events that are part of any family. Author Anne Bernstein observes that, after having their own baby, stepmothers tended to "lighten up," becoming "less jealous, more empathic, and less critical of their stepchildren."[5] She explains that "because their self-esteem is less tied to their effectiveness as a stepparent, they are less focused on finding fault and less emotionally reactive to the older children's misbehavior."[6]

Stepmothers seem to enjoy their family more after the birth of the new baby. But what effect does the baby have on the stepchildren? This will largely depend on the stepmother's attitudes and actions. The following recommendations should help to foster love between the stepchildren and the new baby:

1. *Express your love for the stepchildren before the baby is ever born.* A lot of the adjustments to the new baby depend on the prior relationship between stepmother and stepchild. A new baby won't fix a hostile relationship; it may worsen it. But a new baby may deepen an already healthy affection.

2. *Balance the needs of all the children.* Newborns take a *lot* of time and attention, but *not all* of a mother's time and attention. Remember to maintain a genuine interest in the other children. June and William Noble wrote that "apparently children aged four to twelve have the most difficult time adjusting [to a new baby]. This is a vulnerable period, and it's full of insecurities."[7] Little children may watch their stepmother dote on a newborn and ask themselves, "I wonder if it would be different if I were her 'real' child?" Though a new mother may be tired from delivery, from lack of sleep, and from the constant care given to a newborn, she needs to actively reassure her young stepchildren of her love for

them. This is a time for patience, for listening, for playing, and for hugging!

As you raise children, some are more demanding than others. Try to pay attention to all the children, but recognize that life is never "fair." You can rarely do the exact same deed for two children. Love all your children, step and natural. Do your best to include everyone but don't become obsessed with equity. Claire Berman describes "being fair" as making sure if something is bought or done for one child the exact thing must be done for the others. She notes that "because this calls for constant assessment of the equities of each situation and doesn't permit for spontaneous, natural action, this may be the most unfair of all approaches."[8]

**3. *Involve the older stepchildren in child care.*** Bonding between the stepchildren and the new baby can occur before the baby is ever born. I remember Kay and David putting their hands on my tummy to feel the babies move. How they laughed! They anticipated these babies too!

David and Kay were eleven and twelve years old when Amy and April were born. At first, I was so nervous that I didn't want anybody to pick up my five pound babies! However, soon reality set in, and I realized I needed all the help I could get! David and Kay were *wonderful* help! They rocked, fed, and entertained their tiny baby sisters for me, easing my load considerably. They became a second set of parents to Amy and April.

Kay recently told me: "I think I was excited the most when I found out that you and Dad were expecting. I was finally going to stop being one of 'the babies of the family.' However, it wasn't simply that. It was exciting just to have the babies come. I remember watching your stomach grow (and grow and grow and grow) with anticipation. We all talked about baby names, watched the active babies play at least three separate sports at one time while confined in their chambers, and watched the office/study change into a nursery.

"It was a thrilling 2:00 A.M. wakeup when I was told that Dad was taking you to the hospital. I remember anxiously awaiting the call to tell me that I had twin sisters. They were full sisters in every way that counted with me. I wanted to do everything: feed, burp, dress, babysit, change diapers. I'm sure that I was underfoot a lot at first, but I guess persistence helped. I soon had as much work as I wanted. And I did love it. I do want to stress that I adore my sisters."

Some stepchildren feel abandoned after the birth of a new baby. Involving them in caring for the baby is a good antidote for these feelings. Don't coerce the older children to help but encourage them. As stepchildren share in the baby's care, a deeper bond is formed with their stepmother as well.

When Ruth brought her new baby boy home from the hospital, she wanted her young stepsons to feel included in the event. She took a number of pictures of the older boys holding the baby and then she gave each stepson a present from the baby. The boys were thrilled to be such an important part of the day!

**4. *Encourage a direct relationship between stepchild and mutual child.*** As the mother and stepmother, you do not need to control the relationships your children develop. Sometimes staying out of the way is healthiest. As Bernstein noted, this "permits them to feel like brother and sister, rather than adversaries in a struggle for limited parental love."[9]

I have a favorite photograph, a picture taken of David holding the handles of an old wheelbarrow. In this wheelbarrow are two blonde toddlers, squealing with delight after being given a bumpy ride around the backyard by their big brother.

I have another snapshot memory from the early years. I can still see Amy, about three years old, standing in front of

Kay's mirror, brushing her thin wisps of blonde hair with great vigor. She wanted to be just like her big sister Kay who had long, thick, shining hair. Kay provided a strong, loving role model for her little sisters. Amy took on many of Kay's mannerisms when she was little and, happily, grew to adopt Kay's Christian values as well.

Even to this day, there is a special relationship between Amy and April and their older brother and sister. They make specific plans to spend time together, even though all of their lives have become so busy. One recent college spring break, April flew to Montana to spend a week with David and his family, while Amy flew to Kansas to share the week with Kay and her family. All of the children enjoyed those seven days of catching up on each other's lives.

David's concern for his younger sisters was vividly expressed with a phone call he made when Amy and April had just left for their first year of college. Their departure was a major adjustment for me, the first time in my married life that I would have no children at home. Don and I were both adjusting to a very empty nest. When David called, he wanted to know how I was doing, if I had heard from Amy and April, what they said, and how they were getting along. He ended our conversation with a wonderful question. It spoke volumes about his relationship with Amy and April when he asked, "Mom, is it possible for an older brother to experience the empty nest syndrome?"

Adding babies to our stepfamily brought happiness to us all. They drew us even closer together as members of a family born of loss. Instead of loss, we now experienced new gain. Amy and April's birth was an unspoken but unmistakable announcement that we were moving forward as a family.

# ELEVEN

# Phases of Our Family's Life

*I see not a step before me as I tread on another year; But I've left the Past in God's keeping,—the Future His mercy shall clear; And what looks dark in the distance may brighten as I draw near.*

**—Mary Gardiner Brainard**

SOMEONE ONCE SAID that constant change is here to stay. I confronted the reality of change on a recent visit to Southern California where I lived just three years ago. On a nostalgic drive through my old neighborhood, I was amazed to see numerous houses standing on what had been vacant lots. A nearby shopping center was completely leveled and new structures were under construction. A favorite restaurant was gone. The landscape had changed significantly.

Life is change and life in a stepfamily is no exception. A stepfamily will always be a stepfamily but it will always be in transition. This has certainly been true in my own experience.

Recently I charted the past twenty-three years of my marriage on a single sheet of paper in order to have an overview of my stepfamily's life. I found this exercise to be very helpful in gaining insight into phases and dynamics of our family's life. If you have been married for ten years or more, this exercise could be helpful to you too.

In the first column, I wrote the calendar year. In the next few columns I wrote my age and the ages of other family members for that year. Then I recorded significant life events, particularly events in the lives of the children. Looking at this chart, I easily observed four distinct phases in our history as a stepfamily: 1) The first three and a half years were years of rapid change with older children leaving and new babies arriving; 2) The next five years were years of identity achievement as a stepfamily; 3) For the next eleven years, my husband and I parented a nuclear family with only our two mutual children still living at home; and 4) for the past three and a half years, we have lived in an "empty nest."

## 1. THE EARLY YEARS

The first few years of my married life required the most adjustments and were therefore the most stressful. Don and I married, honeymooned, celebrated New Year's Day with the children, and returned to our teaching jobs, all in one week. Two months later, Don's oldest son Rick came home to stay with us for two short months before he enlisted in the Marine Corps. Soon after, I quit my job to become a full-time homemaker and to concentrate on the needs of my new family. That spring, Sharon was graduated from high school, heading off to college that fall. That left only three stepchildren in the home—Steve, Kay, and David. The following spring, Amy and April were born into our family, bringing the number of children at home back to five. That summer, we left New York and moved to Colorado. Two years later Steve was graduated from high school and launched out on his own, marking the end of this first phase of our family's history.

All three older stepchildren were launched during our first three and a half years of marriage. I married their father at the time when these children were being weaned from the family and finding a new sense of independence. In Ralph Ranieri's guidebook for stepparents, he urges the stepparent of an adolescent to "join in the process of letting go. This may be difficult because the natural reaction of someone entering a family is to take hold rather than let go. But the entrance of a stepparent into the family should not hinder the adolescent's development."[1] The first three children were ready to separate from the family and explore adult independence. Separation was psychologically healthy for them as well as for those of us remaining at home.

Some stepmothers live for the day when adolescent stepchildren move out of the home and begin lives of their own. This is true when the children are particularly resentful about their father's remarriage. When the hostilities remain unresolved, the departure of these stepchildren precipitates relief from ongoing tension. Though the immediate tensions abate, stepmothers still hope for better feelings with these children. There is reason to hope that these feelings will improve. Often, as young people experience adult realities, old hostilities fade and are replaced by a more empathic understanding of the stepmother's challenging role.

Rick, Sharon, and Steve lived with us for a very small portion of our married life: Rick, for only two months; Sharon, for eight months, and Steve, for three and a half years. Acknowledging the brevity of their life in our home helps me to place my relationship with them in clearer perspective, establishing more realistic expectations, and producing an "attitude of gratitude" for the affection we share.

This is the case in my relationship with Rick, Don's oldest son who is only two and a half years my junior. I liked Rick right from the start, but he lived with us a very short time and after that lived out of state. We never had much time together to get to know one another, but when Rick phones, we enjoy talking to one another and catching up on news. It would be extremely unrealistic to hope for more than a good friendship with Rick, but we're both convinced that the friendship we enjoy is worth celebrating. Cherie Burns puts it this way: "Too often we focus on what the relationship isn't instead of what it is. The likely friendships and affection pale in comparison to impossible expectations for a mother-and-child bond. The contrast is unfair. It is a very fine thing to be a good friend to your stepchild, but if you expect to love and be loved like a mother, you may find friendship an unsatisfactory substitute."[2]

If you are a stepmother who entered your husband's life when his children were almost grown, patiently strive to be a friend to them. Give them and yourself time to know one another. Be content to develop a relationship of mutual respect, and should friendship, or even love, grow out of that respect, consider yourself all the more blessed. Realizing that each child deals with the stepfamily in his or her own way will help a stepmother be content with differing levels of acceptance and intimacy with her stepchildren. Typically, stepmothers feel closer to some of their stepchildren than to others. While they work to establish healthy relationships with all the stepchildren, they should not be surprised if this is easier to accomplish with some of the children than with others.

Not only were the three older stepchildren launched during this first phase of our marriage, but the two youngest children were born. The birth of twin daughters into the family created happy but substantial changes. Amy and April became a key ingredient in the transition to the next phase of family life. They symbolized that we all belonged to one another in a new and tangible way. Their birth paved the way to solidifying our family's new identity.

## 2. FAMILY IDENTITY ACHIEVEMENT

With the departure of the three older children, our family consisted of Don and me, Kay and David, now two teenagers, and Amy and April just two years old. All of these four children now conceive of this configuration as their primary family unit. Don and I felt secure in our marriage, routinely operating as a team. Roles were clearly defined and practiced.

A sense of family identity was expressed in the fact that now, for the first time, all the children called me "Mom." This had always been important to Kay and David. They felt that when the older children called me by my first name it was a statement that we weren't entirely a family. During this second phase of our family's life, which lasted just five years, we all operated within clearly defined roles. There was a father, a person that *every* child related to as mother, and four children. My role was now commonly perceived and experienced by the children. Calling me "Mom" was their symbolic and unifying stamp of approval.

At the close of this second phase Kay and David were graduated from high school and began their undergraduate studies at the local state university. They were close enough to home to visit often and to celebrate holidays for the next few years, but they were clearly launched into their young adulthood. Their departure marked another dramatic change in our family's experience.

## 3. A PRIMARILY NUCLEAR FAMILY

For the next eleven years, almost half of my married life, our family predominantly functioned as a nuclear family. Don and I were never out of touch with the older children, who all married and became parents themselves, but our day to day lives were focused on the nurture of our own two daughters. From elementary school through high school, we enjoyed watching Amy and April grow from little girls into energetic young adults.

Though, of course, I remained a stepmother during this period, that role was no longer central to my life. With only two daughters at home, our home life became less complicated and therefore less stressful. Release from the demands of caring for a large household was a blessed relief.

As Amy and April matured, I found new freedom to pursue personal goals outside of my family responsibilities. For me, this meant more education. During this phase of family life, I earned a seminary degree and a doctorate in education. Our family of four moved to California where Don assumed a new faculty appointment and where I began a new career as a seminary professor. Developing a role apart from mothering was helpful in adjusting to the final phase of our family's life.

## 4. THE "EMPTY NEST"

Two years after moving to California, and soon after Amy and April graduated from high school, our family moved back to Colorado so that Don and I could assume new professional responsibilities. I joined the faculty of another seminary and he established a private practice in educational diagnostics.

Moving meant gain, but it also meant loss. We left behind wonderful friends, enjoyable jobs, a fine church, and a sense of the familiar. And the day we moved, our dog died. Just two months after landing in Denver, I found myself facing the empty nest. Amy and April, the last two of the seven children, were heading back to California to start college. I was flooded with an overwhelming sense of loss.

The day the girls left for college is burned into my memory. Don and I knew it was going to be emotionally tough. We anticipated the scene at the airport when Amy and April would say their goodbyes, board the plane for what would feel like forever, and when we would crumble in a devastated heap of abandoned parenthood. I hated to think about it.

When that warm, late August day finally arrived, the four of us headed to the airport. Amy and April were conspicuously animated as they anticipated their first year of college. Don and I, in contrast, felt subdued. We arrived at the airport, checked in the luggage, and headed to the gate. After a strained forty-five minutes of waiting, it was time for the girls to board. We hugged each other hard and said what felt like sudden goodbyes. In an instant my children were gone.

I felt this big hand take hold of mine as Don and I headed down the concourse alone. I didn't look up for a few seconds. When I did look up into Don's face, he was grinning from ear to ear, and so was I! We'd been caught off guard by an unexpected new sense of freedom and exhilaration! For the first time ever, we were just a couple with no children to build our schedules around. How strange... how wonderful!

We missed Amy and April very much and were always eager for their weekly phone calls and news about college life. But to the girls' relief, as well as ours, we found the "empty nest" to be great fun! The "empty nest," best interpreted, is a statement that the parent birds have completed their responsibilities and taught their young to fly. It is a powerful symbol of accomplishment. Even when parents are disappointed in the values and lifestyles of their launched adult children, the "empty nest" marks the moment when their primary parental responsibility has come to its natural conclusion. This realization, in itself, brings resolution to the parent and freedom to move on with life.

My roles as wife and seminary professor gave continuity to my life as an "empty nested" mother. Amy and April's departure for college could have been extremely painful if I had limited my roles to stepmothering and mothering. Those roles were gratifying and important, but not sufficient to sustain a sense of well-being after the children were grown. Stepmothers need to cultivate personal interests outside of their family that will enrich their lives, give them a sense of continued purpose, and ease their transition into the empty nest.

## LIVING WITH CHANGE

Each phase of a stepfamily's life is important. As I review my own stepfamily's history, I'm grateful for the difficult times of adjustment—the demands for personal change that deepened my spiritual life and fostered personal maturity. I never ask for pain, but I appreciate its function in my life. A farmer once told me that his corn always grew faster at night. The corn absorbed nourishment from the sun during the day, but grew in the dark. We need the nights of our lives as stepmothers.

I am encouraged by the sunnier days of our family's life as well. Each one of my children has brightened my life. Looking back over all the years of our family's life, I would choose the same family all over again. We have grown in our understanding of each other and ourselves. We have learned to be friends. We have learned to love. We have sensed the hand of God guiding and strengthening us as we learned how to be a family.

How can stepmothers whose lives are constantly changing learn to live with the changes?

1. *Accept change.* Your life as a stepmother cannot remain the same. Your husband will change, your children will change, and you will change. Trying to hold onto circumstances as you know them now will only frustrate you. Don't

fight change, join it! Change can be welcomed as a friend. It may bring trials, but it also brings triumphs. Above all, change calls us to God. When we are alone with God, we can review our personal history and the changes in our life as a stepfamily and seek God's direction for the future.

**2. *Step into life by faith.*** The great patriarch Abraham accepted the challenges of enormous change *by faith!* In Hebrews 11:8 we read that, "by faith Abraham, when called to go to a place he would later receive as his inheritance, obeyed and went, even though he did not know where he was going." The detailed account in Genesis 12 records how God asked Abraham to leave behind all that was familiar to him—his homeland, relatives, and home and to set out for an unknown, unseen promised land. Stepmothers launch out into uncharted territory. Their journey is not usually as drastic as Abraham's, but it nevertheless requires faith. Life ahead will be full of difficult challenges and unforeseen changes.

Sometimes women say, "I don't know if I have the strength." They are probably right. The encouraging ingredient in Abraham's biography is that he began his journey at the age of seventy-five! Where did he find his strength? He found it in God! Abraham arrived at Shechem and built an altar to the Lord (12:7) and then he moved on to Bethel where he built another altar to the Lord (12:8). After journeying through Egypt, he returned to Bethel and to the altar where he again called on the name of the Lord (13:4). After dividing up the land with his nephew, Lot, Abraham moved on to Hebron, and there built another altar to the Lord. This was a man, *enabled by his confidence in God's presence,* who moved ahead through the challenges of many changes!

**3. *Celebrate God's immutability!*** When I have gone through periods of heightened change and demanding adjustments, as in the early phase of my life as a stepmother, the truth of God's immutability, his unchanging nature, has brought me great comfort. His promise is: "I the LORD do not change" (Mal 3:6). In Hebrews 13:8, we are promised that "Jesus Christ is the same yesterday and today and forever." When life gets stormy in our stepfamilies, we can anchor our hope in God's sovereignty. He knows, he reigns, and he doesn't change. He is the reliable certainty, no matter what.

When children left home, when babies came, when finances were stretched, when illness threatened, when we moved—whatever the changes that we faced as a family— we knew that, like Abraham, we could move ahead, aware of God's faithful presence. A relationship with an unchanging, loving God is the secret to handling change. Then, as stepmothers we can enter our role into the promise of Psalm 9:10: "Those [stepmothers] who know your name will trust in you, for you, LORD, have never forsaken those [stepmothers] who seek you."

**4. Concentrate on your mission for today.** Jesus taught us how to establish life's priorities, thereby handling the stress of anticipated change. While delivering his Sermon on the Mount, he told his disciples not to fret about their material needs but to "seek first his kingdom and his righteousness, and all these things will be given to you as well" (Mt 6:33). He continued, "Therefore do not worry about tomorrow, for tomorrow will worry about itself. Each day has enough trouble of its own" (6:34). Jesus taught us to concern ourselves with how we live today, how today might count for eternity.

What is it that you can do as a stepmother *today* that will please God? What deed of kindness, word of encouragement, or specific task is God requiring of you? How can you best spend your today so that God will be honored in your life as Mom No. 2? Don't waste today. A wise person said that "What I do today is important because I'm exchanging a day of my life for it." Your role today as Mom No. 2 is vitally important to you, to your husband, to your stepchildren, and to God!

# TWELVE

# A Cord of Three Strands Is Not Quickly Broken

*A stepmother is the key to the stepfamily, and she is the most likely member of the family to seek help. If she can understand and deal with particular problems of individuals living "in step," her family will have a much better chance.*

**The Good Stepmother: A Practical Guide**
**Karen Savage and Patricia Adams**

WHEN SHE REMARRIED and became Mom No. 2 to her husband's three children, author Karen Savage also brought her own two children into the new family. An instant family of seven was born with many new relationships to be formed. Determined to beat the odds, her new family hoped they could find happiness together. She writes, "it could only have been hope that propelled us forward into the unknown experiences of a stepfamily."[1] Stepfamilies are a living testimony to hope. Second marriages proclaim that, in spite of the pain from past loss, there is hope for future joy.

The Christian woman's hope for a future as Mom No. 2 rests in her growing awareness of the reality of God's steadfast presence in her life. As the psalmist David came to understand, so, too, will Mom No. 2 realize that life is fleeting.

It's all too easy to waste life when driven by empty goals like keeping busy and accumulating wealth (Ps 39:4-6). David framed the *key* question when he asked: "But now, Lord, what do I look for?" Mom No. 2 must also ask the same question. She, like David, must ask, "What will be the focus of my life?" The only true answer to this essential question is David's pronouncement: "My hope is in God" (Ps 39:7). Mom No. 2's only hope for a meaningful future is a walk with God. The writer to the Hebrews describes this wondrous hope as an "anchor for the soul, firm and secure" (Heb 6:19).

Jesus Christ is our hope. Hope is the heart of the gospel message. Because Christ paid the penalty for our sin at Calvary, we are promised the forgiveness of sins, a restored relationship with God, a mission for this life, and eternal hope. Our part is to repent of our sins, accept these promises, and give Jesus his rightful place as Lord in our lives.

This hope of the gospel is realized *in community* with other Christians. When we embrace this hope, we are called to be humble, gentle, and patient with others, working together to preserve the unity of the community of faith (Eph 4:1-6).

Hope is not fleshed out in isolation! God's people become *channels of hope* in each other's lives. We need each other to survive the challenges of life. When we try to "go it alone," we often sink in the mire of disappointment and disillusionment. Mom No. 2 may try to go it alone but will soon discover that she needs other people to help her.

Unfortunately her real need for supportive relationships runs counter to the culture in which she lives. Well-known sociologist Robert Bellah and his associates document the central threads of individualism and its ensuing isolation that are woven into the fabric of American life. Americans want to work out their own lives privately, striving for personal identity, achievement, and fulfillment, negotiating personal happiness on their own terms. Bellah writes: "American cultural traditions define personality, achievement, and the purpose of human life in ways that leave the individual suspended in glorious, but terrifying, isolation."[2]

For all too long, psychologists have defined emotional and social maturity in terms of individual autonomy—a sense of one's self and the ability to handle life independently. In the past few years, however, researchers have challenged these models of autonomy as deficient and suggested that maturity may be better understood as *interdependence*. They are coming to understand what the Bible has always taught—that we need each other. We need to build one another up, encourage one another, and bear one another's burdens.

This means that Mom No. 2 will need to reject the valued individualism of American culture and plug into a reliable support system. The Bible teaches that "two are better than one" and pities "the person who falls down with no one to help him or her up!" (Eccl 4:10). This pity extends to the stepmother without a support system. How sad for women to face the many challenges of stepmothering with no one to lift them up when they start to fall. Two are better than one, but there is even greater strength with three: "A cord of three strands is not quickly broken" (Eccl 4:9-12). Mom No. 2 needs the support of others. To whom can she turn for help? Who can offer hope for the task?

## HUSBANDS

People have often asked me what I would say if one of my daughters told me that she wanted to marry a widower with five children. My counsel to her would include an honest appraisal of the challenges and enormous responsibilities of being Mom No. 2. We would talk about the work, the lack of privacy, the struggle to define her role in the home, and all the other issues stepmothers face. We also would talk about the rewards of loving and being loved by her husband and caring for his children. Ultimately, I would encourage my daughter to take the step only if the man she wanted to marry were as kind and gentle as her father.

My experience as Mom No. 2 has been very rewarding, but I am convinced that this is true because my marriage has been so happy. Don did not marry me to give away his parental responsibilities to someone else. He married me because he loved me and wanted to build a life together. I had his full support from day one.

The stepmothers who seem most secure about helping to raise their husband's children are those who are happiest in their marriages. A supportive husband is the indispensable ingredient in Mom No. 2's personal sense of well-being. Cherie Burns underscores the husband's role: "A husband determines much of his wife's stepmothering experience. If the children are beastly but he is involved and supportive of her, she will find that stepmothering isn't so bad. It works the other way too. If the children are angelic but he is an ineffectual ally, she may well find stepmothering a misery.... A stepmother can botch a few things on her own but she cannot be successful, even at her very best, without her husband's support."[3]

Mom No. 2's husband needs to be a good listener, a participatory parent, a friend, a lover, and a spiritual partner. She needs to be able to confide in him and to feel encouraged by him. Anne, stepmother to four girls, usually turned to her husband when she needed help in her relationship with his daughters. She and her husband then usually turned to God together. Anne remembers that they prayed, and prayed a lot! In prayer, they were drawn closer to God and to each other, and they found renewed commitment to loving the children.

Sometimes, the second marriage has occurred too quickly after the end of the first marriage. The husband is feeling too vulnerable and guilt-ridden himself to be of much comfort to his new wife. As stepfamily experts, Emily and John Visher, comment: "Frequently, guilt, anger, and disappointment result in anxiety and low self-esteem. It is very difficult to give emotional support to others when you are feeling empty and in turmoil. Since everyone in a new stepfamily may be experiencing considerable emotional pain at the same instant, there tends to be little support and validation available within the family system."[4]

When everyone in the stepfamily is first adjusting to each other, Mom No. 2 may find more support and objective counsel from people outside the family. Sometimes her husband is part of the problem; sometimes he is the very one that causes her to feel closed out of the family unit. Even when new stepmothers feel very close to their husbands, they often hesitate to discuss the children, especially conflict with the children. When this is the case, stepmothers definitely need to seek support outside of the family.

## FRIENDS

A dear stepmother, now in her seventies, told me that she got the most help from her friends at work. She said, "I found out that my stepkids were often no different than the natural kids of my friends. That made me relax!" Another stepmother agreed. Her women friends at work shared about their children and they agreed that all parents are challenged, not just stepparents.

Women friends listen to each other, help each other, nurture each other, and instill confidence in each other. Friendships help Mom No. 2 cope with her new identity. Trustworthy friends provide a safe place to share struggles. George Eliot voiced this eloquently by saying: "Oh, the comfort, the inexpressible comfort of feeling safe with a person; having neither to weigh thoughts nor measure words, but to pour them all out, just as they are, chaff and grain together, knowing that a faithful hand will take and sift them, keep what is worth keeping, and then, with the breath of kindness, blow the rest away."[5]

Stepmothers need someone who will listen to their anger on a particularly stressful day, someone who will hear their hurt, someone who will listen to their "unacceptable feelings" nonjudgmentally, and then will "blow the chaff away." They need a friend to laugh with, to cry with, and to pray with. Friends can make the difference. They are God's dynamic channels of hope into the everyday circumstances of Mom No. 2.

In my first two years as a stepmother, I didn't know any other women who were stepmothers, nor about any books on the subject. I needed a friend, and God provided Marilyn. She was a few years older than I, married, and a mother. She was my "safe place." She was a good listener and a marvelous encourager. Marilyn was also a professional pediatric nurse, and soon after my twin daughters were born, she practically pushed me out of the house on a date with my husband. I found it hard to leave my babies with someone else for the first time, but Marilyn insisted and then gave of her time to care for the babies. She was a good friend.

During most of my child-rearing years, God provided women with whom I prayed on a regular basis. I will always be grateful for my friendships with Naomi, Joyce, Janie, and Florence. They were all prayer warriors. We shared our concerns about our families with each other and we gave those concerns to God. Our friendships became a source of tremendous nurture and growth. We not only prayed together, but we learned together, worshiped together, and played together. I am not sure how women survive the tests of parenthood without the love of good friends. The strong bond I felt with these women is my most convincing personal evidence that "a cord of three strands is not quickly broken."

## SUPPORT GROUPS

Those women who could best understand Mom No. 2's emotions and challenges would likely be other stepmothers who have faced the same adjustments themselves. While all of our friends can offer support, only other stepmothers can fully identify with our questions about how to survive and succeed as Mom No. 2.

John and Emily Visher, after forming a stepfamily together and researching the dynamics of stepfamily life, saw a need for stepparents to support one another. They formed the Stepfamily Association of America, headquartered in Baltimore, Maryland. This organization is divided into local chapters across the country and provides an opportunity for stepparents to meet regularly, share their own stories, and help each other to cope with adjustments unique to stepfamilies.

Not long ago, my pastor lamented from the pulpit that so many hurting parents in the church insist on keeping their pain to themselves. When they struggle with their children, they call the pastor for help. Yet they refuse to give him permission to put them in contact with other hurting parents. The pastor wanted our congregation to know that there are many families hurting in our midst. The best thing we could do would be to share our needs with each other and to encourage each other!

Perhaps your community does not have a support group for stepparents. Don't overlook the possibility of beginning one in your church! The church, with its commitment to the hope of the gospel, should be the first place where stepparents can go for help. This means that we must take off our masks of maternal bliss and admit that we need help as Mom No. 2. The church must open its doors to the wounded, be committed to those who are hurting in their family life, and be willing to listen and willing to help.

If your church is small, you might consider cooperating with other churches in the area in forming a community support group. These support groups are a tremendous source of encouragement; their very existence reassures Mom No. 2 she is not alone in her struggles. Support groups provide a confidential setting in which she can share her frustration, her anger, her lack of confidence, and her fears. She can also learn from others how to overcome her negative emotions. Practical suggestions from other stepparents will ease her frustration. She will find that she is able to help others as well, that she has become a vehicle for hope to other stepparents.

Christian support groups provide an opportunity for stepmothers to study God's Word and to pray. They become a place of spiritual, emotional, and practical encouragement. When we come together as Christian stepmothers, we admit our fundamental need to know God and to seek his will for our lives, including our parental roles. When we come together in prayer, we understand that God is big enough to strengthen us for our task as Mom No. 2. Our prayers are no longer, "God get me out of this mess!" but, rather, "God, empower me to be the best Mom No. 2 that I can be. Help me to show your love through me!" Support groups are the embodiment of the biblical commands to bear each other's burdens and to build each other up, thereby glorifying God!

## PROFESSIONAL HELP

Sometimes the stepfamily's history and interpersonal dynamics seem particularly hard to understand. Many stepmothers have sought professional help in clarifying their role in the family and in understanding how to help their family.

Sometimes, a sense of personal failure and guilt can keep Mom No. 2 from seeking professional help, but these are the very feelings that should drive her to get it! Family counselors can bring objectivity to a stepmother's feelings about her new role and help her understand the contribution that she can make to the family's physical, emotional, and spiritual health.

Diane's stepchildren had suffered so much. Their natural mother was an unhappy woman and unable to give her children the attention they needed, so the children learned to care for themselves as best they could. Though their mother had neglected them, the children loved her very much. When she died, they were devastated. When Diane unexpectedly became stepmother to these little children, they were angry and out of control. Diane knew she needed professional help. She was wise enough to see that she and the children had major adjustments ahead. She recalls, "I wanted to change things, behaviors and attitudes, at a fundamental level."

Diane contacted a therapist whom she knew and respected. The therapist met with Diane and her husband as a couple and then worked with the children. The process of grief recovery for the children was slow and painful. Learning to adjust to their new life as a stepfamily was hard work. However, the entire family was helped by the counseling sessions and eventually learned how to live together with less stress and greater satisfaction. Diane was perceptive enough to see the wisdom and strength of her decision to enlist the help of a professional. She told me, "It's weak *not* to admit you need help!"

Nancy has remained in counseling even after her husband refused to go anymore. She says, "I'm learning how to care for myself emotionally." In these trying times when, not only her stepchildren are rejecting her, but her husband as well, this is important to her. Counseling affords Nancy the opportunity to talk about her painful feelings of isolation and confusion. Her counselor is helping Nancy figure out how to survive emotionally from day to day.

## OUR PLACE OF PERFECT REFUGE

Nancy, though contending with a hostile and unloving family, knows her source of ultimate hope. She says with calm assurance, "My strength comes from the Lord."

Jesus promised to be with those who love him (Mt 28:20). He sent his Spirit to be our comforter and to empower us to live a Christian life, empower us to live a Christian life as Mom No. 2! The Apostle Paul's prayer for the Ephesians (Eph 3:16-21) is my prayer for all Mom No. 2s. I pray that you may know the power of the Holy Spirit, that you may be rooted in God's love, that you may grasp how fully you are loved by God, and that you may know him "who is able to do immeasurably more than all we ask or imagine" (v.20). I pray that your life as Mom No. 2 may bring glory to God forever!

Committing your life to God is no guarantee of an easy life. In fact, your troubles may increase. Pain is unavoidable in this life, but the Christian knows the hope of God's presence in the midst of painful circumstances. Perhaps you are discouraged, like Nancy, and are wading through the deep waters of an unloving stepfamily. If so, your greatest comfort can be found in God's presence—our place of perfect refuge. Though you may not know joy in your marriage or with your stepchildren, you can know the joy of God's faithful presence. Put your life into the words of the psalmist and feel God's protection and care for you:

> But let all [stepmothers] who take refuge in you be glad;
> let them ever sing for joy.
> Spread your protection over them,
> that those [stepmothers] who love your name
> may rejoice in you.
> For surely, O Lord, you bless the righteous [stepmothers];
> you surround them with your favor as with a shield.
> —Psalm 5:11,12

# THIRTEEN

# A Little Money and Great Wealth

*Keep your lives free from the love of money and be content with what you have because God has said, "Never will I leave you; never will I forsake you."*

**—Hebrews 13:5**

IT'S BEEN SAID THAT STEPFAMILIES never have enough time, money, or bathrooms.[1] Stepchildren live with the daily reality of divided parental attention and an acute shortage of bathrooms, but they may not realize the financial dimensions of stepfamily life to the degree that adults do. For Mom No. 2 and her husband, money problems may grow like uncontrollable weeds, choking the very life out of their new marriage.

While most failed second marriages end over disagreements about children, financial stress comes in second as a cause for marital breakup. Money, or the lack of it, and attitudes about money can do great harm to the emotional stability of a stepfamily.

Most families struggle with money problems. Usually, people feel they have too little money and worry about how they will pay their bills; sometimes they struggle with too much money and worry about how they will protect their investments. Either way, they have missed the key to under-standing the place of money in their lives.

When the Apostle Paul wrote to his young disciple Timothy, he warned him about the devastation that comes from loving money: "... The love of money is a root of all kinds of evil. Some people, eager for money, have wandered from the faith and pierced themselves with many griefs" (1 Tm 6:10). Building a life around the acquisition of material wealth can lead you away from a relationship with God and result in bitter and empty disappointment. Instead of pursuing money, Paul gave Timothy the formula for achieving great wealth. He spelled it out clearly and succinctly when he said: "Godliness with contentment is great gain" (1 Tm 6:6). As pastor and author Chuck Swindoll comments: "This formula for success would never make the cover story of *Forbes* or *Money* magazines. The great wealth spoken of here is a wealth that rust can't destroy or thieves steal (Mt 6:19-20). A consistent and authentic walk with God plus an attitude of inner peace... that's what constitutes great wealth."[2]

If stepfamilies want to resolve their conflicts over money, they're going to have to sort out their feelings about it. Is acquiring more money the most important part of their lives, or are they most concerned about knowing, loving, and obeying God? Have they learned to be content with what they have? The secret is "being content in any and every situation, whether well fed or hungry, whether living in plenty or in want" (Phil 4:12). Godliness and contentment are the formula for great wealth, eternal wealth that money can't buy. It's clearly possible to have very little money and enjoy great wealth!

## LEARNING TO LIVE WITH LESS

While the income level of a stepfamily may sometimes go up after the marriage, usually it goes down, particularly if both partners bring children to the second marriage. This means that Mom No. 2, her husband, and the children have to learn to live with less.

Most stepfamilies in our country today are formed through divorce and there are significant financial costs accompanying it. Legal fees and the costs of dividing a household can be staggering, seriously depleting assets acquired in the first marriage. Worse yet, a divorcing partner may need to borrow heavily to pay court costs and may still be paying on these loans at the time of a second marriage.

Sometimes, Mom No. 2 must live with less because her husband is sending alimony checks to his first wife. Unless she accepts this reality from the beginning of her marriage, it will gnaw away at her and breed a bitterness that will only threaten her chances for happiness and her family's happiness.

Child support payments put additional strain on the stepfamily. Mom No. 2 must watch the family income be divided between two households. Some is allocated to support her and perhaps some mutual children, and some is given to support her husband's children from his first marriage, who are likely living with their natural mother most of the time. Child support payments can also eat away at Mom No. 2's ability to be content, but she must get a grip on this additional financial reality. Child support is a Christian duty. Her husband has a responsibility to all his children, not only emotionally and spiritually, but financially. He must help care for their physical needs.

Money can be used as a weapon in stepfamilies, particularly where healing from a prior divorce is not complete. A mother may say, "I'd like to buy you that, but your father didn't send enough money." A divorced father who has not come to terms with the guilt he feels over the breakup of his marriage may overindulge his children when they are with him. He may spend money he shouldn't spend to compensate for his feelings of failure as a father. His spending can be very upsetting to Mom No. 2 who is acutely aware of the needs of her own children.

Child support payments and the limits of spending for visiting stepchildren should be handled by the divorced parents. The children should not be brought into these discussions. Child support is a business arrangement established by the courts. While most divorced fathers fail to make these payments, Christian divorced fathers should take this responsibility seriously and have the encouragement of Mom No. 2 to meet their parental financial obligations.

Joan and Craig have a modest income but a big stockpile of emotional contentment. They are happy to own a small house, to have warm and comfortable clothing, and to have enough to eat. When Joan's stepchildren are with their natural mother, they are given designer clothes and the latest in teen-age fashion accessories. Joan and Craig, financially unable to provide those things, make no apologies. They understand the kind of great wealth that they give to their children, the eternal wealth of Christian values taught and lived out in their home. Joan could let Mom No. 1's indulgences upset her, but instead, she's decided to model contentment in learning to live with less.

KEEPING NO SECRETS

When their love relationship becomes serious and marriage is first discussed, every prospective husband and wife needs to be completely honest about his or her personal finances. Though not always easy, this disclosure is essential to financial harmony. Sharing financial secrets after marriage is too late and may put the second marriage in immediate jeopardy.

Only when both marriage partners have a realistic financial picture can they determine whether or not they can meet their financial obligations. The stepfamily's goal should be freedom from debt, and this can only happen when a plan is developed using honest figures. It would help a couple to discuss previous spending habits—where they tend to overspend, what they hate to spend money on, where they feel money must be spent.

## PLANNING YOUR FINANCIAL FUTURE

Together, *before their wedding,* marriage partners should develop a realistic budget for their new family. If they need help, they should enlist the expertise of a financial counselor who can help them learn to live within their means, work to pay off debts, and set aside some money for the future, as well as meeting current expenses. This budget should reflect their family's Christian values, including a regular tithe to support the ministry of their local church as well as other organizations whose work they deem valuable.

The Christian family's budget should reflect a concern for the poor. As much as the stepfamily may feel confined by limited income, the poor among us face the brutal realities of hunger, disease, and cold nights without adequate shelter. One Christmas, my husband and I explained to our children that our household budget was tight, and though we'd be celebrating Christmas happily, we would be exchanging fewer gifts than in some previous years. To our amazement, joy, and *shame,* the children began to remind us of all that God had provided for our family. They suggested that this would be the perfect time to take on the support of a child with far less. That Christmas, out of gratitude for God's abundant provision and recognizing his love for the poor, we assumed the sponsorship of a child in a third world country. For approximately twenty dollars a month, we were able to express our family's concern. That budget item became a catalyst for a growing concern for the poor. Our children taught us a valuable lesson that Christmas. Families, including stepfamilies, can do something to help those in need.

One budget item the stepfamily should not overlook is adequate health insurance for all of the children. Parents need to work insurance needs out with ex-spouses if they are in the picture to be sure that each child is covered by a parent's policy.

Budgets can make a positive contribution to the emotional stability of the stepfamily. One stepmother, who lived with the strain of a rebellious stepson, found the realities of her household budget very helpful in dealing with money issues as Mom No. 2. She and her husband worked out a household budget together and were both committed to living within its limits. When her stepson asked for more than they could provide, she answered honestly and without guilt, "No, I'm sorry, but we can't afford that." It's never easy to say no to a child, but a defined budget makes it easier. Her stepson often complained, but she knew that living within their means was her family's only ultimately satisfying choice. Overspending would have brought frustration, worry, and conflict.

Mom No. 2 and her husband also need to prepare a will. A will is especially important when there are small children in the home, as this instrument allows parents to designate who would care for the children in the unlikely event that both parents should die. Developing a will is an emotionally sensitive process for anyone, but may even be stickier for Mom No. 2. One stepmother confessed, "I want to do more for my own children. I feel bad saying it, but it's true. My husband warned me that I'd feel this way—that I'd feel differently about my own children than about his children. In our will, however, we treated the children equally. My husband feels that all the children are his and should be treated the same, and that's okay."

Estate planners find that there is more conflict among surviving children over possessions than over cash. However you decide to bequeath your financial assets, Mom No. 2

and the children's father should ask each child if there are particular *things* that they would especially want to inherit. Parents may be surprised at those items that have special meaning to their children. Designating specific gifts to each child could spare the stepchildren a great deal of unnecessary and painful conflict in the event of the parents' death and these gifts may become a lasting symbol of their father's and Mom No. 2's concern for them.

A *mutual* financial plan with agreed on financial goals helps Mom No. 2 and her husband deepen their commitment to their future. Responsible money management is an important part of faithful Christian stewardship and says a great deal about their commitment to biblical values.

## YOUR MONEY, MY MONEY, OR OUR MONEY?

Money represents emotion. It can symbolize feelings of power and trust. When Laura married John, she became a full-time homemaker in order to focus her attention on raising her stepsons and managing the home. She and John opened a joint checking account, and Laura used that account to pay the monthly bills. She recalled that her stepsons "didn't like me to have control of the checkbook." They saw her access to their Dad's income as power that they didn't want her to have. Money became a symbol of their stepmother's parental role, a role they resisted. When Laura was out shopping one day, one of her stepsons explained her absence by saying to a friend, "Oh, she's out spending my Dad's money again." That assessment hurt Laura. She and her husband viewed his earnings as family income, not just her husband's income. Sharing the checkbook was a statement of their mutual trust and commitment. Financial decisions were mutual; money was not a power issue in their marriage, but became a power issue in Laura's relationship with her stepsons.

The basic question in managing money in the stepfamily is whether or not to have a "common pot" or "two pots." This decision is particularly difficult for stepfamilies born of divorce. After a divorced parent has agonized with the financial costs and hassles of a broken first marriage, there is understandable reluctance to establish a "common pot" in the second marriage. This reluctance reflects a lack of trust in the stability of the second marriage because of the disillusionment experienced in the loss of the first marriage.

Some stepfamilies decide to have two separate sets of financial books. This occurs most often when both parents have been divorced, both are working outside of the home, and both have children to support. The husband supports *his* children and she supports *her* children. This arrangement can work and does work sometimes, especially in situations where the parents' income is at about the same level. More often, the "two pot" approach doesn't work because it communicates a basic lack of trust and works to polarize members of the stepfamily.

The healthiest approach to money management still appears to be the use of the "common pot." Authors and stepmothers Elizabeth Einstein and Linda Albert observe that: "With the common-pot approach, couples pool resources and distribute them according to need, not blood ties. Adults avoid distinguishing between *yours* and *mine* and do away with extra bookkeeping. This method reflects a high level of trust and commitment to the family. Remarrieds who manage money in this way report family unity and a positive attitude about the future of their stepfamily."[3] When Mom No. 2 and her husband develop a budget together, see whatever income they earn as shared, and give each other access to the checkbook, they are communicating mutual care and trust.

So much of what we know is easier said than done. I laugh now at my early hangups over money during my first year of marriage. When I married Don, I was teaching high school and he was teaching at the university. His income was significantly higher than mine, but both paychecks went into a common account which we used to pay our family bills. Somehow, the fact that I contributed to our earnings made me comfortable in spending money from our mutual account. My problem surfaced after I decided to quit teaching and stay home with the children full-time. I had difficulty seeing Don's income as "our money."

When our first Christmas rolled around, it didn't seem right to buy him a Christmas present with "his money," so I decided to get a temporary job at a local department store where I had worked summers during my college years. Taking a job during the Christmas rush would help out my old boss and also allow me to earn enough money to buy Don's present with "my money." My biggest problem was that *I* was big. I was pregnant with twins. When I applied for the job, the store manager who happened to be a good friend, agreed to hire me for a couple of weeks. "But," he said, "you're so pregnant, I'm only willing to use you in the candy department. That way, you can pretty much hide behind the candy counters where people can't see most of you, just your head."

Don wasn't pleased that his pregnant wife wanted to go back to work, but he reluctantly agreed. I took the job, but only lasted one week. The overwhelming, sickeningly sweet aroma of fudge, mint, hard candy, butterscotch, toffee, caramel, and all the other confectioneries gave me a powerful reoccurrence of morning sickness! I felt queasy all day long all week, but I earned a small paycheck and used the entire amount to buy a present for my husband for Christmas.

We have laughed at my foolishness many times since. That one experience and some kind, but firm, reassurances from my husband, convinced me that whatever income God provided for our family belonged to the entire family, not just the one who worked outside of the home. Actually, it's amazing just how easy it became to shift my thinking from "his money" to "our money" after my short career as a nauseous, pregnant candy salesclerk!

## SPENDING WHERE IT COUNTS

Whatever income God provides, the Christian stepfamily will want to invest all of their resources, finances, time, and energy, in eternal values, seeking first to let God and his Word rule in their lives. Money is not trustworthy. The Bible warns us of its transient and unreliable nature:

> Do not wear yourself out to get rich;
>    have the wisdom to show restraint.
> Cast but a glance at riches, and they are gone,
>    for they will surely sprout wings
> and fly off to the sky like an eagle.
>      —Proverbs 23:4, 5

Jesus told us not to chase after and worry about material concerns, but to be concerned about the kingdom of God, to focus on obeying him. As he preached his powerful Sermon on the Mount, he told his disciples not to store up earthly treasures that can rot or be stolen, but to store up heavenly treasures than can never be destroyed (Mt 6:19-21).

Mom No. 2 should strive to be responsible in managing what money God provides. She should encourage careful investment in her family's needs—her own needs, her husband's needs, and the needs of all of the children. She should encourage the investment of family monies in Christian ministries beyond the scope of her family's outreach. Most important, Mom No. 2 should invest her whole life in extending the kingdom of God, in witnessing to God's goodness and kingship, no matter what her financial circumstances.

# FOURTEEN

# The Stepmother's Survival Kit

*In every heart He wishes to be first:*
*He therefore keeps the secret key Himself*
*To open all its chambers, and to bless*
*With perfect sympathy, and holy peace,*
*Each solitary soul which comes to Him.*

**—Anonymous**

L ET ME SUGGEST THAT EVERY STEPMOTHER pack a survival kit for her journey through the unknown terrain of life as Mom No. 2. If I could pack this kit for her, I would include at least four critical tools necessary for her survival—time, tolerance, rest, and solitude.

## TIME

I'd pack in a generous portion of time because there's no way to survive as a stepmother without it. Adjusting to life as Mom No. 2 is a major and complex change for any woman and she won't have figured out "how to be a stepmother" by the time she arrives home from her honeymoon.

By packing lots of time in her survival kit, I'm encouraging her to use it wisely, but not to panic by thinking she's living on a meager supply, nor to grasp frantically for unattainable instant success as Mom No. 2. I want her to feel she can give herself this gift of time, moving slowly and learning what it means to be a loving stepmother one day at a time.

## TOLERANCE

She'll need a good dose of tolerance, too, for a satisfying journey as a stepmother. Mom No. 2 typically thinks in terms of tolerating the weaknesses of others—her husband, her children, and her stepchildren. She tells herself to overlook their foibles, forgive their insensitivities, and to focus her attention on the central family values that matter most.

Somewhere in her concern to forgive others, however, she has overlooked her need to forgive herself. Can she learn to tolerate her *own* human failings? Can she give *herself* the freedom to fail? Can she accept God's forgiveness and learn to forgive *herself*? I'd like to pack an extra portion of tolerance into Mom No. 2's survival kit, so she'll feel free to use some of it for herself. I've learned from personal experience the necessity of self-tolerance.

Kay and David were completing college and living at home off and on. Amy and April were in fourth grade and at school most of the day. Raising my family no longer took as much of my time, and I began praying about what God would have me to do with my life. I wanted to know what ministry he had for me next.

Through a process of searching, praying, and listening, God led me to pursue a seminary education. As a former schoolteacher, I had a heartfelt concern for educational ministry in the local church. I knew that the church was in need of people to train teachers, helping them learn how to communicate God's Word more effectively. With tremendous encouragement and support from my husband and my church, I launched into a master's program in Christian Education. The closest seminary was sixty-five miles from my home, which meant that, in addition to keeping up with my studies, my time would be absorbed by a substantial commute. "Not to worry," I told my family. "I can handle this; everything will go on just as before. I can do it all."

Before school started, I made a lot of extra casseroles and put them in the freezer so I'd have something to use for supper on nights when I was especially tired. I thought through how I could manage my time as a wife, a mother, an active church member, and a student. No problem.

Wrong—big problem! I found that I was exhausted every night. After two and a half hours of driving, and after spending time taking notes in class, reading and taking notes in the library, and studying every minute I could at home, I found that I was getting worn out. I quickly used up my prepared casseroles, the dirty laundry was piling up, and I was not "handling it."

One afternoon, after a particularly stressful exam at school, after cramming in the library and driving an hour and fifteen minutes home, I walked through the back door, threw my books onto the kitchen table, and fell like a lifeless lump into the nearest chair. Just as I landed, Amy and April came bounding up the back steps and into the kitchen. Usually, they were animated and anxious to share all the news of their school day. Usually I greeted them with an after school snack and a listening ear. Not this day. There was no snack ready, I was feeling too tired to listen to anybody, and they were clearly upset by some trauma germane to being in the fourth grade.

Amy and April started in, pouring out their little girl troubles. "I'm sorry," I said. "I'm too worn out to handle this right now." I quietly left the kitchen, headed for my bedroom, disappeared into my walk-in closet, and sat down on a substantial heap of dirty clothes in the corner. I didn't even turn the closet light on. Surrounded by a mound of laundry, I sat there in the dark and cried like a baby. More than just landing in a pile of laundry, I had landed in the pile of my own compulsions—my need to "do it all," to "handle it," and "to do it all well." As I sat there in the dark crying, it became clear to me that my life needed some serious adjustments.

Isn't it amazing what it takes to push us to moments of enlightenment like that? After I stopped crying, I faced the reality of my new commitments. I was trying to do too much, I was trying to do it too well, and I was trying to do it by myself. These things had to change.

That evening, I talked about my feelings and frustrations with my husband. He was glad for my confession and had been worried about my adjustment to the demands of graduate study. It was time for the two of us to rethink our commitments and priorities. We both agreed that our spiritual life and our family life were most important, and we both agreed that God had provided this opportunity for seminary training. We just needed a new strategy for coping with its pressures.

We began by agreeing that it was good to live simply. It wasn't necessary to prepare the time-consuming meals that I used to fix before I became a student. We would eat nutritiously, but simply. Don offered to cook some of our dinners. We agreed to overlook a little dust and clutter and to clean the house together on Saturdays. With our children, we listed the tasks required to keep the house running, and they chose ways to pitch in and help. I taught my ten-year-old daughters how to sort and wash their own laundry. They learned to do this willingly and did a very fine job. My family encouraged my educational goal in tangible ways, by pitching in and taking on more responsibilities at home. My demanding schedule drew us closer together instead of driving us apart.

REST

In addition to learning to prioritize, simplify, and share the load, I learned another very important lesson about myself that day. I learned how easy it was for me to neglect my need for personal rest. Because of my training and temperament, I felt compelled to make every minute count. My daily schedule was packed with things to do. I was in desperate need for both rest and solitude.

By relaxing my standards for household cleanliness, and actually discovering that no one would die if we only vacuumed once a week, I found that I was far less stressed and was given the gift of more time. I needed to use some of that time to *rest*—not to study, not to clean, not to drive, not to run errands, not to check something more off my "to do" list.

I had to teach myself to rest. I began by scheduling mini-vacations for myself every day, at least one a day. A mini-vacation was a period of time that was purposely set aside for rest. It usually lasted about half an hour, during which I could relax in any way that I wanted. Sometimes I would read a women's magazine purchased at the grocery store. Sometimes I would fix a cup of hot tea, curl up in an over-stuffed chair, and just daydream. Sometimes I would watch a half hour of television. I "wasted time" with no guilt, because I had planned to waste time. Of course, I soon learned that these were times well-spent, and that after I had taken a few moments of rest, I was ultimately able to accomplish much more in much less time during the remainder of the day.

Mom No. 2 needs to evaluate her time. How does she plan her day? Are there any moments set aside for her to sit and rest? Or does every moment have to result in some tangible accomplishment—laundry done, kitchen cleaned, letter written, phone call returned?

For Mom No. 2 to find the strength to serve her family, she

must allow herself the joy of personal rest. Regularly scheduled moments of rest are not a luxury; they are essential.
When God gave the law to Moses, he instituted a day of
rest—a Sabbath (Ex 20:8-11). God wanted a day set aside to
worship him and a time when his people would rest from
their labor. God told Moses that the Sabbath was to be a
"sign between me and the Israelites forever, for in six days
the LORD made the heaven and the earth, and on the seventh
day he abstained from work, and rested" (Ex 31:17). Mom
No. 2 will find her role more satisfying as she applies the
principle of Sabbath rest to her own life, taking moments
apart to be refreshed.

## SOLITUDE

Solitude is probably the piece of equipment in Mom No.
2's survival kit that gets the least use, simply because she
doesn't know how to use it. I use my computer almost every
day. I use this wonderful machine as a word processor, a
marvelous improvement over the typewriter I used for so
many years. But I know that my computer has many other
capabilities of which I do not take advantage because I don't
understand how to use them. Solitude is like that. We don't
understand the nature and role of solitude in our experience
as Christian stepmothers, so this tool lies idle in our survival
kit. This neglect of solitude is a tragedy, because it's our most
powerful weapon against discouragement and defeat.

Solitude means taking time for spiritual renewal. It does
not mean being alone; it means being alone with God. The
first thing that Mom No. 2 must do is to find a regular time
and a place to be with God alone. She must commit herself
to spending time in his presence, listening to his voice
through his Word, conversing with him in prayer, and being
silent before him. This commitment to the spiritual discipline

of solitude is difficult to sustain against the force of the "hurry up and rush" realities of our daily life, but solitude is the secret to endurance, meaning, and joy in life. Only when we become quiet before God can we evaluate our lives, sorting out what's really worth doing. Author and theologian Henri Nouwen describes our empty "busyness" well: "... we move through life in such a distracted way that we do not even take the time and rest to wonder if any of the things we think, say, or do are worth thinking, saying or doing. We simply go along with the many 'musts' and 'oughts' that have been handed on to us, and we live with them as if they were authentic translations of the Gospel of our Lord."[1]

Solitude provides us those moments to evaluate the "musts" and "oughts" and to ask God if they are from him. As we read God's Word, we come to understand his desires for our life. We come to understand what really matters.

When Mom No. 2 talks with God in prayer, she discovers that God is her refuge and strength. She can tell him everything that is on her heart—her discouragements, her questions, her fears, as well as her joys, and hopes, and desires. She can discover the strength and indescribable peace that come from praise and thanksgiving (Phil 4:4-7). She can pray with the psalmist David (Ps 51:10-12):

Create in me a pure heart, O God,
and renew a steadfast spirit within me.
Do not cast me from your presence
or take your Holy Spirit from me.
Restore to me the joy of your salvation
and grant me a willing spirit, to sustain me.

In prayer, Mom No. 2 can strengthen her resolve, renew her joy, change her attitude, and find power. She can be healed of her sorrow and pain and deepen her faith in a sovereign God.

It's not important that we pray like a saint, that we master the poetic prayers of the professionals. All that matters is that we come to God openly and honestly, confessing to him who we really are and seeking to know, love, and obey him.

I love old books, and a few years ago I purchased a volume entitled *The Royal Path of Life,* a book about moral values written more than a hundred years ago. In its pages I found a marvelous commentary on prayer: "God respecteth not the arithmetic of our prayers, how many they are; nor the rhetoric of our prayers, how neat they are; nor the music of our prayers, how melodious they are; nor the logic of our prayers, how methodical they are—but the divinity of our prayers, how heart-sprung they are."[2]

Let your prayers spring from your heart. Take time to talk with your God.

Not only is solitude a place of restoration but, more importantly, it is a place of confrontation. When we are alone with God we can no longer rely on what Nouwen calls the "scaffolding" in our lives—friends, telephone calls, meetings, music, books.[3] Without these distractions, we confront our own vulnerability and sinfulness. In God's presence, we learn to set aside our own agendas; we abandon our need to "look out for Number One." We learn to set aside our selfish needs and to be filled with the presence of Christ. Mom No. 2 can abandon her need to be the family's heroine, savior, or center of attention, and instead say with the Apostle Paul, "For to me, to live is Christ" (Phil 1:21).

When Mom No. 2 opens her survival kit and takes hold of solitude, she will grow into a woman of deep compassion. Nouwen writes that "solitude molds self-righteous people into gentle, caring, forgiving persons who are so deeply convinced of their own great sinfulness and so fully aware of God's even greater mercy that their life itself becomes ministry."[4] When Mom No. 2 experiences the reality of God's love and compassion, she becomes his minister of that love and compassion in the lives of her husband and stepchildren.

## A GREATER PERSPECTIVE

Catching a glimpse of God's perspective helps us live a more meaningful life. The tools in Mom No. 2's survival kit are for her ultimate benefit. The Bible tells us that our life on earth is fleeting, just "a mist that appears for a little while and then vanishes" (Jas 4:14). We are on this planet for just a short gasp of breath in the infinite expanse of eternity (Jb 7:7). God has entrusted us with our brief moments on earth and we need to be faithful stewards of that time. Loving life means turning from evil and doing good; seeking peace and pursuing it (Ps 34:12-14). Choosing life means loving God, listening to his voice, and holding fast to him (Dt 30:19, 20). When we see time as a *resource* to be used for God's glory:

1) we will not begrudge using **time** to build relationships within our stepfamilies;
2) we will see our personal growth as Mom No. 2 as a *process*, as we develop over time, and exercise more **tolerance** of our setbacks;
3) we will understand the benefit of using time for personal **rest** and renewal; and
4) we will pursue **solitude**, desiring more time alone with God.

The pilgrimage of a stepmother's life can be a satisfying adventure even when the road is difficult. The joy of the journey does not come from the absence of challenge but from meeting that challenge with time, tolerance, rest, and solitude.

# FIFTEEN

# The Ministry of Stepmothering

*Parents need only to do their best and trust God to do the rest... All that God asks of parents, as they try to help the children of the blended family grow in love for one another, is that they be faithful to the task and continue to love. Whether they are successful or not isn't always something that can be measured. Leave that part in God's hands.*

**The Blended Family: A Guide for Stepparents**
**Ralph F. Ranieri**

THE HEART OF JESUS' MINISTRY was summed up by his disciple Peter's words in Acts 10:38: "He went around doing good." John Stott, British pastor and author, reminds us that Jesus "told us to follow his example, and to show our love for our neighbor by doing good, by serving him in some practical and positive way."[1] Stepmothering is an ideal opportunity to do good and to serve in practical and positive ways.

Knowing God's unconditional love for us frees and empowers us to love others (1 Jn 4:19) and to love our stepchildren in particular. And as Stott says so well, "Divine love is service, not sentiment."[2] The Bible says, "Let us not love with words or tongue but with actions and in truth" (1 Jn 3:18). Fulfilling our role as a stepmother means sharing God's love in our *actions* toward our stepchildren.

When we hear the word "ministry" we too often think of the professional ministers who study at Bible colleges and seminaries and then take paid positions in the local church. Jesus defined ministry in a very different way. He showed his disciples what he meant by ministry in one profound act; he washed their dirty feet (Jn 13:4-17). At the Last Supper, soon before Jesus was to die on the cross, he got up from the table and girded himself with a towel, the dress of a servant. Then he knelt and washed the disciples' dirty feet. When he finished, he told them to follow his example.

There are "dirty feet" all around us. So many people are hurting and in need of help. Many of these "dirty feet" are in our own families.

Sociologists have labeled the next future generation of young people "The Angry Generation." These will be the children of divorce, the children who have suffered great loss and pain when their families broke apart, and who have never recovered. Losing a mother, through death or divorce, leaves a child feeling desolate, distraught, and often angry. Stepmothers are the women God can use to wash the "dirty feet" of these children of loss, to help heal their wounds and to turn their anger to peace. Stepmothers are God's ministers of his divine love, the women he calls to put his love into action.

## CHOOSING TO SERVE

Joyce, whose stepsons visit every other weekend, put it bluntly: "I can *choose* to minister to these children or to be selfish. Sometimes it's easy to think 'they're doing fine with their mother. She takes them to church.' But I want to do better than 'getting by.' I must *choose* to make an effort—to pray for them, to plan their weekend visits carefully, to fix up their bedrooms for them." Women do have a choice. They can simply endure their stepchildren until they become independent adults, or they can actively love their stepchildren by serving them.

I appreciated Evelyn's candor when she told me, "The first year was not a ministry. It was a war zone! Seeing stepmothering as a ministry has been a process for me. I am *learning* to love my stepson and not to be angry." When the angry words fly, when stepchildren wish she would go away, when the work piles up, Mom No. 2 must make an important choice. Will she fight back, withdraw, hoping the problems will all go away, or love unconditionally? The choice is not always easy, but in the end only love works. Fighting only escalates the war; hostilities increase. Withdrawal never makes the problems go away; they only increase. But love "covers over a multitude of sins" (1 Pt 4:8). God's love, active love, wins out over anger and hostility. God's love alone, a love that may be channeled through a Christian Mom No. 2, is the only sure answer to the challenges of a stepfamily.

## A MINISTRY THAT MATTERS

Her appearance was striking, her words articulate, her manner easy. We'd never met before until that morning, but after an hour of good coffee and warm conversation, I knew I'd met a great lady. She'd married a widower, raised his two children as well as two of their own, and was about to send her youngest off to college. It was clear that she took her ministries as a stepmother and mother seriously and that she had established good relationships with her children. When her eyes suddenly filled with tears, I was caught by surprise.

She told me that her youngest daughter, while looking through college catalogues recently, voiced her disappointment in a mother that had never gone to college. Then the daughter had asked, "Mom, what have you done with your life anyway?" The words of that question stung like poison and this mother could not let go of them.

We talked about that question together. What had she done with her life? As we talked, she said quietly, "God put me in this family and I think he put me here for a purpose. I wanted my family to be my ministry. I wanted to be a witness to my children." She had answered her own question! Having a life that counts has nothing to do with academic accomplishments, or monetary worth, or social status. Having a life that counts has everything to do with obedience! This wonderful lady had followed God's leading and given her life to the care of those who needed her. She had a powerful ministry in her own family!

## HOW TO HELP AS MOM NO. 2

Every stepfamily is unique. Mom No. 2 should pray and ask God to help her be sensitive to the needs of her own stepchildren. There is no universal "how to" manual for stepmothers, but the following are avenues of ministry suggested by a number of women out of their own experiences as Mom No. 2s:

**1. *Live a Christian life.*** Show your stepchildren what it means to love and be loved by God. Model a life of obedience and faith before your stepchildren. Show them what it means to live by God's Word.

One stepmother remembered when she and her stepsons shared a poignant lesson about honesty and integrity. She treated her young stepsons to a drive-in movie at a place where children under twelve got in free. Though the older stepson had already turned twelve, he passed for younger, and the family entered without paying for him. Later, back at home, this sensitive Mom No. 2 thought about what they had done and felt convicted. She explained to her stepsons that it had been dishonest for them not to pay, so they wrote a short note to the movie theater and enclosed the five dollars they owed. Five dollars. A small amount, but a big lesson.

**2. Tell your stepchildren the "good news."** The "good news" is that God loves them so much that he sent Jesus to die on the cross for their sins, and to forgive their sins if they will believe in him. The "good news" is the promise of eternal life.

One stepmother said that her husband's oldest son, John, decided he could no longer live with his mother. Mom No. 1 was more lenient with John, but they didn't get along well. Then John came to live with his dad and stepmom. Part of the package in his new home was the expectation that everyone attended church together on Sunday. After some months, John became a Christian. He turned his life over to Christ. Mom No. 2 values this moment in her ministry as a stepmother above all others.

Your stepchildren may not be receptive to the gospel during your first years of marriage. They may not give you permission to talk about their spiritual lives, but you can "live the gospel" for them. You can show them what a life looks like that has experienced God's grace, and you can live that grace out in your family. You can accept your stepchildren and love them unconditionally in the same way that God loves you. In time, you may discover a receptive moment when they'll allow you to talk about the gospel.

**3. Give your stepchildren a good dose of "old fashioned motherliness."** Bake cookies, read stories, plan surprises, fix favorite meals, wash their clothes, have their friends in. Whether your stepchildren live with you part-time or full-time, they will welcome some motherly "Tender Loving

Care." Sometimes we view these gestures as menial but they are monumental. They are God's love in action. The time invested in washing our children's dirty clothes and preparing healthy meals for them is the time when we wear the towel of a servant and wash dirty feet. This is ministry!

**4. *Show them how to have a happy marriage.*** In stepfamilies formed through divorce, the children have witnessed a poor marriage, perhaps an angry marriage. In stepfamilies formed by a death, the first marriage may have been happy, but perhaps it was not. Even if it was happy, children profit from every opportunity they can get to see how a good marriage works.

One Mom No. 2 was concerned about the lingering bitterness on the part of Mom No. 1 towards the divorce. The children, who lived with Mom No. 1 most of the time, were constantly barraged with angry words about their father and stepmother. Mom No. 2 worried about what attitudes the children were forming towards marriage. As she learned to know her stepchildren, she talked with them about marriage and told them honestly, "You've all seen a bad marriage; your dad and I want you to see a good one." They discussed their commitment to the Lord and to each other and how they were learning to love each other more each day. They also put their commitment into practice, respecting and loving each other in day-to-day living.

Another stepmother said that her stepsons were learning that married people can disagree without fighting. These little boys were frightened by disagreement, because it destroyed their father's marriage to Mom No. 1. But in the stepfamily they watched their father and stepmother disagree, talk, and work a problem out without fighting. When they get older and marry, they will have a model for healthy problem-solving in a family.

**5. *Be a trustworthy friend.*** We all need someone we can talk to. We all need someone we can trust. Your stepchildren are no exception. As you develop a relationship with them, keep your promises. And keep their confidences.

**6. *Be kind to Mom No. 1.*** If your stepfamily was born out of the death of Mom No. 1, be kind to her memory. Allow the children to talk about her and don't try to compete with their love for her or their memories of her.

If your stepfamily was born out of divorce, be kind to your stepchildren's Mom No. 1. More often than not, they live with her most of the time and they need to have the best relationship with her that's possible. Regardless of how unkind, mean-spirited, or vengeful she may be towards you or your husband, she is the mother of these children and they need her. Mom No. 1, often deeply wounded by the loss of her marriage and subsequent loss of self-esteem, needs to know the love of God. Perhaps she is so hostile that you can't even have a conversation with her, but you can pray for her and you can refrain from criticizing her in front of her children.

**7. *Be kind to extended family.*** Death and divorce can often separate children from Mom No. 1's relatives. Grandparents especially fear losing touch with their grandchildren. Your first choice may not be to spend time with Mom No. 1's family members, but make the effort for the sake of your stepchildren. Help them cultivate a sense of belonging that reaches beyond their immediate family.

**8. *Help other women who are also Mom No. 2.*** Every Mom No. 2, whether happy or sad in her role, can offer substantial help to other women who are stepmothers. She helps them know that they are not alone, that they share similar feelings, frustrations, failures, and successes. She listens to them, prays with them, and helps them. This makes being Mom No. 2 a lot easier, especially in the hard times. God uses women to minister to other women as emotional, physical, and spiritual caregivers. We need each other! We need to wash the tired, dirty feet of a discouraged Mom No. 2 and we need to have our own feet tenderly cleansed as well.

## "BEING SURE OF GOD'S HAND"

Dietrich Bonhoeffer was a young German theologian, incarcerated for his opposition to the Nazi regime and eventually executed. While in prison he wrote: "I am sure of God's hand and guidance.... You must never doubt that I am thankful and glad to go the way which I am being led. My past life is abundantly full of God's mercy, and, above all sin, stands the forgiving love of the Crucified."[3] His circumstances were not happy; they were difficult. But he could be glad, because he was where God had led him. He was "sure of God's hand!"

Your circumstances as Mom No. 2 may not be happy; they may be difficult. Our culture mistakenly tells us that we have an inalienable right to be happy, but this is not a biblical notion. In fact, the Bible tells us that we may be hated, ostracized, and insulted (Lk 6:22). This can even happen in a stepfamily. We don't want to hear this; we want everything to be happy. Sometimes it isn't.

In trying times, in those times when you may feel rejected and unhappy as Mom No. 2, Jesus' words to you are that you should "do good, and give, expecting nothing in return." (Lk 6:35). As you fulfill this command, living out your life as a loving, giving Mom No. 2, his promise to you is that "your reward shall be great." The Bible encourages us "not to lose heart in doing good, for in due time we shall reap if we do not grow weary" (Gal 6:9).

Your stepchildren may respect you, or not. They may praise you, or not. They may love you or not. More than likely, they will someday thank you for your care for them as a stepmother. But, even if you never hear a word of gratitude, you can know incredible joy as Mom No. 2 by being obedient to the way that God has led you, by being sure of God's hand, by not growing weary in doing good in your ministry as Mom No. 2!

# From the Author's Husband

THE YEAR BEFORE THE DEATH of my first wife was very hard. Our family of seven lived through some tough times with their mother experiencing inexplicable emotional stress. Although there had been inklings of difficulties even before our marriage, this slender, rather withdrawn young woman found herself increasingly engulfed in periodic emotional storms that confused and distressed us, herself most of all. Many evenings I sat with her well past midnight as she wrestled with severe depression and rage until exhaustion brought sleep and relief. At other times, emotional episodes threatened her own well-being or the well-being of the older children.

Although she possessed obvious insight and understanding as she discussed her difficulties with medical specialists, her unexpected eruptions buffeted our family and mystified the doctors whose advice we sought. We tried to downplay her problems as much as possible, but every member of the family was living within the experience, and it profoundly affected and troubled us. Only after her death from a burst aneurysm did we discover the cause of her devastating emotional changes. Her feelings and her behavior had been directly affected by periodic swelling of the aneurysm which exerted pressures within her brain.

Although the year before her death was hard, the time immediately following her death was the most difficult in my life. My first priority was to provide sufficient stability for my children. At the same time, I fought intense personal depression and grief. What kept me going was the God-given necessity of providing for my children. It was an enormous struggle, but a necessary one, and one that I alone could fill. I had to give my children a sense of continuity despite this family tragedy. I knew that without me there was no one to help my kids pick up the pieces and go on. Big things and little things filled my days: big things like trying to make sure that the kids felt safe, that I wasn't also going to disappear, and "little" things like seeing that everyone had enough good food to eat and decent clothes to wear. Knowing that my children had no one else to rely on kept me going. The kids and I were close. We had never needed each other more. Still, it was tough. I don't think we could have made it but for the grace of God.

After surviving those first weeks, I found that bit by bit, every day, or at least every week, existence became a little easier, not *easy*, but eas*ier*. The Lord provided good steadfast friends who helped in many important ways. The staff at the university research center I directed supplied a dozen or so quick casserole recipes which I could put together in the morning after I saw the kids off to school, place in the oven with a set timer, and have ready for dinner when I got back late that afternoon. One good friend from work went shopping for clothes for my youngest daughter, and another friend at church who owned a women's clothing store helped my oldest daughter.

One day another friend showed up at the door with a huge tag board schedule, outlining the daily and weekly household chores with a place to assign them to family members. It was complete with a box of stars to stick on after each chore had been done. What a help it was!

Teachers also helped. My youngest son, David, brought

home a report card that showed terribly poor grades and his teacher expressed concern about work not being handed in. David was a very bright kid; I couldn't figure out what was wrong. I went to school, and his teacher told me that David spent a great deal of time in a kind of daze, not really participating in class discussions and not doing his work. It dawned on me, belatedly, that I had not clued in his teacher that he had lost his mother. I recognized that David was still in the grief process. I talked to the teacher about the death of his mother, and together we decided to simply give him some space to recover. It worked.

Gradually the dynamics of the family improved. We talked occasionally about their mother's death, but not enough. I discovered later that one or two of the children might have benefitted from more planned and therapeutic discussions. Unfortunately, the last few months before their mother's death had been so distressful for all of us that despite the horrible trauma of death, the lack of turmoil and emotional storms that followed seemed oddly almost peaceful. The older two children particularly noticed and commented on it to me. It is not that we did not miss her, terribly, but we had spent months in the eye of an unpredictable emotional storm, and its absence probably misled me, making me think that we were surviving better than we actually were.

At any rate, I began to pull out of a terrible depression and life began to assume some degree of normality. I had to change some of my responsibilities at the university, and Sharon and the other kids all assumed greater responsibility at home. I was terribly proud of them! I'm not sure what would have happened if it had not been for the willingness of Sharon to shoulder so many burdens she shouldn't have had to care about at age 16. She assumed most of the responsibilities.

Although we weren't always sure where God was leading, we were always aware of his guiding hand, particularly after that awful first month. He provided people to help us when things might have completely fallen apart. He even moved three school teachers in across the street because he loved us and cared for us!

I don't want to neglect an important fact regarding the reasons God brought Beth into the family. Although I shall be eternally grateful to God that he gave Beth to us in part to be the mother to my children, the truth is that God's greatest gift to me was Beth as a new marriage partner. She is a vibrant, engrossing, fun-to-be-with, intelligent, life-loving person. While my children gained a mother, Beth made me, and still makes me, fuller, richer, and more complete. She is God's gift to *me*!

I had never enjoyed talking to anyone as much, never enjoyed watching anyone as much, never *enjoyed* anyone as much as I enjoyed Beth! The truth is, I did not and I would not have married Beth to be a mother to my children, thankful as I am that she became that. I married her because of what she became to me. Long after all the kids leave and have their own families, Beth and I will have one another. I won't be married to "Mom No. 2," I'll be married to my first choice of a wife, Beth, my life's companion!

I've been aware throughout my life that I have a tendency to expect less of the Lord than he provides. I realize that God doesn't have a Beth behind every bush, just waiting to help every man who's trying to raise a family any more than there's a Christian man for every woman struggling with the realities of the loss of a husband through bereavement or divorce. However, God really does care for us, forgive us, and supply our every need. Even more, he supplies abundantly.

I know a man, whom I'll call Roger, who lost his wife at the same time I did. Since we were in similar circumstances, we talked together on several occasions. Loss of a spouse is a terrible thing, and Roger took it as badly as anyone I know.

One day, I was surprised to find him to be almost cheerful. He'd found a woman, he said, who reminded him so much of his late wife. He thought they might be able to make a go of it, and then everything would be all right again.

I remember talking to him until I ran out of words, trying to get him to slow down, cautioning him against what he was clearly determined to do, but it was no use. He married a ghost of his wife only to find that she was a very real person with her own needs and her own expectations. Nowhere among those was a need to be Roger's surrogate wife, a substitute for the real thing who was no longer alive. She wanted to be Roger's real wife, his true love, his one and only! Nevertheless, they married, quickly lost their illusions, and the marriage was over before it had well begun.

Roger brought all the baggage, all the expectations, all the troubles, all the ways of doing things from his first marriage into his new one. It didn't stand a chance. But Roger is not so different from the rest of us. Every single parent thinking about remarriage risks doing the same thing. It's possible to lose a spouse and remarry only to find that one or both partners has brought so many old ways of doing things, so many problems, and so many attitudes into the new marriage that it has little chance of survival.

It was a major concern to me that I not do this to Beth. I promised her that insofar as possible she would not have to deal with the "One-Who-Was-Not-There." In some ways, it's difficult to compete with a former spouse and mother who is still living; it's *impossible* to deal with one who is not. The "sainted dead" may assume unassailable heights in recollection; an "honor guard" may form around her memory. The stepmother who chooses to do things differently than the deceased spouse can run the risk of appearing almost sacrilegious.

The one who must be first to counteract this tendency is the husband and father. He must set the tone through direct statement and behavior: Though the family will always love and respect the natural mother, their new stepmother must have the chance to be herself, to do things the way she is comfortable. There will be changes and accommodations, but the father must be a steady support for his new wife or it will be far too easy for children to divide their loyalties and to resent their new stepmother. However, if their father supports his new wife and treats the changes in a matter-of-fact fashion, the children are much more likely to take everything in stride.

Expect adjustments. I had always felt that I was a good disciplinarian, but Beth introduced a calm frankness in discipline unlike mine. I remember watching as she assumed the basic responsibility for disciplining the younger children, wondering whether or not her approach would work well. I was immensely pleased to find that her approach was an improvement over what I had been doing as a single parent!

Not only did I watch what was happening, we talked about it as we talked about everything else. I suppose one of the things both Beth and I have always enjoyed is spending time talking together without interruption. I love to talk with her, and I think that the Lord has allowed us to escape some of the pitfalls of a new marriage through talking one-on-one. We knew that talk doesn't just happen, it has to be planned, especially in the case of a ready-made family like ours, where other things crowd in. Before we got married, we spent hours and hours across a table from one another talking about the things that mattered to each of us. It wouldn't have worked if we had tried to talk at home because the children would naturally have wanted to be included. In order to talk without interruption, we generally went out.

We've continued the practice throughout our marriage, not as some solemn obligation, but because we liked it. We set a goal, which we have more than amply met, of going out to eat together at least once a week. We go alone; if we go out with someone else, that doesn't count. We enjoy nothing more! I'm convinced it's a keystone of the success of our marriage.

When we were first married, our financial situation forced

us to go out for breakfast more often than dinner, but it didn't make any difference. What mattered was that we had uninterrupted time together to talk, and it was great.

While we talk, I learn how Beth feels about important concerns in our marriage. I don't have to wonder what she thinks about family finances, or how the kids are doing in school or at home, or anything else. As we talk, it comes out naturally and easily. Because I know what she thinks and she knows what I think, the Lord has given us a pretty skinny list of misunderstandings.

There are different ways of talking. One way is to view discussion as a contest to see who can get their point across and convince the other that he or she is right. That's not very effective in building a good marriage. Talking about things is an important avenue for growth. Sometimes I'm sure Beth realizes she's hearing me say the same thing for the tenth time in a row, but she listens anyway. Conversation is a process, a good way to mull things over, to make some good changes, to work things through, and to finally arrive at a conclusion. I try to do the same thing for her, to listen and support, to be a good sounding board.

Our story may sound like some sort of cookbook: If you just do this or that, and stir in a pinch of love, everything will be all right. Of course, that's not so. One of the many important things the Lord has taught us is that without him there is little hope, but with him there is hope and love and good direction for our lives.

Before Beth and I were married, I used to do psychological counseling. After an individual or couple told me why they had come to see me, I usually said something like, "You don't know the answer to your problems or you wouldn't be here. What may surprise you is that I don't know the answers either. However, we both know someone who does, and that's God himself. Let's ask him to guide us, and together we'll find the answers only he can provide." That's the way it has been with our marriage. There have been plenty of times when we haven't known the answers, but we've always known the One who could help us find them.

Beth and I are both committed to working out the problems and to making our marriage succeed. There have been tough times, but we haven't wavered in our dedication to this goal. I feel that even our dedication to one another and to our marriage has been a gift from the Lord, something he has given us as we have stood before him as his children.

The truth of the matter is, God has greatly blessed Beth and me! He has guided us when our natural instincts would have caused us to make serious mistakes. He has given us blessings of unexpected patience and love, and the determination to make ours a godly home. God bless you as you earnestly seek the same for your marriage!

# Notes

## Introduction

1. Paul Cullen, "Stepfamilies: the Growing Majority," *Marriage and Family*, vol. 72, no. 5, (May, 1990) p. 18.
2. David Mills, "Stepfamilies in Context," in *Relative Strangers; Studies of Stepfamily Processes*, ed. William R. Beer (Totowa, NJ: Rowman and Littlefield Publishers, 1988) p. 1.
3. Cullen, p. 18.
4. Frank Furstenberg, "The New Extended Family: The Experience of Parents & Children after Remarriage" in *Remarriage and Stepparenting: Current Research and Theory*, ed. Kay Pasley and Marilyn Shinger-Tallman (New York: Guilford Press, 1987) p. 44.
5. David J. and Bonnie B. Juroe. *Successful Stepparenting*. (Old Tappan, NJ: Fleming H. Revell Company, 1983) p. 19.
6. Claire Berman, *Making it as a Stepparent: New Roles/New Rules* (New York: Harper and Row, Publishers, 1986) p. 5.
7. Elsa Ferri, *StepChildren; a national study*. (Windsor, Berkshire: NFER-NELSON Publishing Company Ltd., 1984) p. 117.

## Chapter One
### The Wicked Stepmother

1. Emily B. and John S. Visher, *Old Loyalties, New Ties*. (New York: Brunner/Mazel Publishers, 1988) p. 3.
2. Marilyn Coleman and Lawrence Ganong, "The Cultural Stereotyping of Stepfamilies" in *Remarriage and Stepparenting:*

*Current Research and Theory*, eds. Kay Pasley and Marilyn Shinger-Tallman (New York: Guilford Press, 1987) p. 20.
3. Juroe, p. 18.
4. Karen Savage and Patricia Adams, *The Good Stepmother: A Practical Guide*. (New York: Crown Publishers, 1988) p. 183.
5. Jesse Bernard in *Remarriage and Stepparenting: Current Research and Theory*, p. 21.
6. Berman, p. 37.

### Chapter Two
### *Twenty-One and the Mother of Five!*

1. Cullen, p. 20.
2. Ibid., p. 21.
3. Cherie Burns, *Stepmotherhood*. (New York: Harper and Row, Publishers, 1985) p. 35.

### Chapter Three
### *Born of Loss*

1. James D. Eckler, *Step-by-Stepparenting* (White Hall, Virginia: Betterway Publications, Inc., 1988) p. 20.
2. Cullen, p. 18.
3. Ferri, p. 10.
4. Ibid.
5. Jeffry H. Larson, James O. Anderson, and Ann Morgan, *Workshop Models for Family Life Education: Effective Stepparenting* (New York: Family Service America, 1984) p. 2.
6. Mills, p. 23.
7. Ibid.
8. Ibid., p. 24.
9. Burns, p. 57.
10. June and William Noble, *How to Live With Other People's Children* (New York: Hawthorn Books, Inc., 1977) p. 21.
11. Cynthia Lewis-Steere, *Stepping Lightly* (Minneapolis: CompCare Publications, 1981) p. 43.
12. Eric E. McCollum, "Love me, love my kids?," in *New Choices* (July, 1990) p. 95.
13. Juroe, p. 19.

14. Visher, p. 92.
15. Ibid., p. 110.
16. Larson, pp. 36-37.
17. Jamie Kelain Keshet, *Love and Power in the Stepfamily* (New York: McGraw-Hill Book Company, 1987) p. 88.
18. Juroe, p. 39.
19. William A. Price, Joseph J. Shorokey, and James J. Enyeart, "Children of Divorce" in *Postgraduate Medicine*, (August 1983) p. 93.

## Chapter Four
### *Love Me Tender, Love Me Now*

1. Ralph F. Ranieri, *The Blended Family: A Guide for Stepparents* (Liguori, Missouri: Liguori Publications, 1987) p. 11.
2. Burns, p. 6.
3. Ranieri, p. 23.
4. Patricia Lee Papernow, "The Stepfamily Cycle: An Experimental Model of Stepfamily Development," in *Family Relations*, vol. 33 (1984) pp. 355-363.
5. Burns, p. 17.
6. Savage and Adams, p. 104.
7. Ranieri, p. 20.
8. Mills, p. 105.
9. Lewis-Steere, p. 59.

## Chapter Five
### *Candlelight, Kisses, and Kids:*
### *Early Adjustments in the Stepfamily*

1. Richard A. Gardner, quoted in Claire Berman, *Making it as a Stepparent: New Roles/New Rules* (New York: Harper and Row, Publishers, 1986) p. 12.
2. Noble, p. 4.
3. Berman, p. 4.
4. Mills, p. 22.
5. Emily B. and John S. Visher. *Step-Families; Myths and Realities* (Secaucas, NJ: The Citadel Press, 1979) p. 47.
6. Burns, p. 69.

### Chapter Six
### Mom No. 2 Is a Married Woman

1. Elizabeth Einstein and Linda Albert, *Strengthening Your Stepfamily* (Circle Pines, Minnesota: American Guidance Service, 1986), p. 29.
2. Keshet, "The Remarried Couple" in *Relative Strangers, Studies of Stepfamily Processes*, pp. 30-31.
3. Burns, p. 38.
4. Einstein and Albert, p. 29.

### Chapter Seven
### Your Place or Mine?

1. Charles Cerling, *Remarriage* (Old Tappan, NJ: Fleming H. Revell Company, 1988) p. 97.
2. Einstein and Albert, pp. 6-7.

### Chapter Eight
### Before I Came and Now That I'm Here

1. Cerling, p. 25.
2. Lewis-Steere, p. 50.
3. Einstein and Albert, p. 8.

### Chapter Nine
### Loving Enough to Discipline

1. Juroe, pp. 141-142.
2. Noble, p. 3.
3. Lewis-Steere, p. 23.
4. Berman, p. 127.
5. Juroe, p. 54.
6. Noble, p. 40.
7. Burns, p. 110.

### Chapter Ten
### And Babies Make Nine...

1. Berman, p. 105.
2. Ibid.

3. Furstenberg, p. 44.
4. Savage and Adams, p. 152.
5. Anne C. Bernstein, *Yours, Mine, and Ours: How Families Change When Parents Have a Child Together* (New York: Charles Scribner's Sons, 1989) p. 122.
6. Ibid.
7. Noble, p. 169.
8. Berman, p. 58.
9. Bernstein, p. 139.

### Chapter Eleven
### Phases of Our Family's Life

1. Ranieri, p. 31.
2. Burns, p. 16.

### Chapter Twelve
### A Cord of Three Strands Is Not Quickly Broken

1. Savage and Adams, p. 10.
2. Robert N. Bellah, Richard Madsen, William M. Sullivan, Ann Swidler, and Steven M. Tipton, *Habits of the Heart* (New York: Harper and Row, Publishers, 1985) p. 6.
3. Burns, p. 16.
4. Visher, *Old Loyalties, New Ties*, p. 31.
5. George Eliot in *The Treasure Chest,* compiled by Charles Wallis (New York: Harper and Row, Publishers, 1965) p. 102.

### Chapter Thirteen
### A Little Money and Great Wealth

1. Visher, *Old Loyalties, New Ties,* p. 102.
2. Chuck Swindoll, *Strengthening Your Grip: Bible Study Guide* (Fullerton, CA: Insight for Living, 1989) p. 29.
3. Einstein and Albert, pp. 33-34.

### Chapter Fourteen
### The Stepmother's Survival Kit

1. Henri Nouwen, *The Way of the Heart* (New York: Ballantine Books, 1981) p. 10.

2. T.L. Haines and L.W. Yaggy, *The Royal Path of Life* (Houston: Lone Star Publishing House, 1881) p. 549.
3. Nouwen, p. 15.
4. Ibid., p. 22.

### Chapter Fifteen
### The Ministry of Stepmothering

1. John R.W. Stott, "Jesus Teaches Us Compassion" in *Compassion Update* (Sept/Oct 1990) p. 5.
2. Ibid., p. 4.
3. Dietrich Bonhoeffer, *The Cost of Discipleship* (New York: Collier Books, 1963), p. 17.